Voilà! 3

GWEN BERWICK AND SYDNEY THORNE
SERIES EDITOR: JULIE GREEN

Clair

Published in 2005 by:
Nelson Thornes Ltd
Delta Place
27 Bath Road
CHELTENHAM
GL53 7TH
United Kingdom

05 06 07 08 09 / 10 9 8 7 6 5 4 3 2 1

A catalogue record for this book is available from the British Library
ISBN 0 7487 9148 5

Series editor: Julie Green

Illustrations by Mike Bastin, Beverly Curl, Mark Draisey, Ian F. Jackson, Nigel Kitching, kja-artists.com, David Russell

Page make-up by eMC Design, www.emcdesign.org.uk

Printed in Croatia by Zrinski

Acknowledgements

The authors and publisher woud like to thank the following people, without whose support they could not have created *Voilà! 3 Clair*:

Claire Bleasdale, Teresa Huntley and Stephen Jones for detailed advice throughout the writing.
Steven Faux for providing the music and songs, with Julien Rose, Alice Gonneau, Lucie Deglane.
Rachel Wood for editing the materials.
Marie-Thérèse Bougard for writing the material for pages 85 and 99 as well as for her detailed advice on language and cultural matters.

Front cover photograph: f1 online/Alamy, by Udo Frank.

Alexandre Valadares-Kaiser, Axelle Bourry & Karline Minelli, their families and friends for the exceptional help they gave to create the photographs. Also, Monsieur Garcia, the staff, pupils and families of College St Pierre; Thierry Plumey and pupils of IUT, Troyes and all the businesses that provided locations and without whose help this project would not have been possible.

With thanks to the following for permission to reproduce coyright material:
EA Games (p71)
Éditions Chanticler (p51)
France Télévisions (p19)
Groupe TFI (p19)
Microsoft Corporation (p71)

Recorded at Air Edel, London with Philippe Smolikowski, Juliet Dante, Marvin Dez, Elodie Laval, Manon Riouat, Sarah Duru, Julien Rose, Alain Stachewsky; produced by Colette Thomson for Footstep Productions Ltd.; Studio Engineer Will Reid Dick

Welcome to Voilà! 3 Clair

- In *Voilà! 3*, you'll meet these three people:

> Salut! Je m'appelle Sadiq. J'habite à York, en Angleterre. Kévin est mon correspondant français.

> Bonjour! Je m'appelle Kévin, et j'ai 14 ans. J'habite à Biarritz, dans le sud-ouest de la France.

> Salut! Moi, c'est Estelle, et j'ai 14 ans aussi. Je suis la sœur jumelle de Kévin!

- **Most pages have the following features to help you:**

  Grammaire:
  Examples of how you put French words together to make sentences.

  A list of the key words and phrases you'll need to do the activities.

  Stratégies!
  Tips to help you learn better and remember more.

  🔘 Activities in which you'll listen to French.

  💬 Activities in which you'll practise speaking French.

  📖 ✏️ Activities in which you'll practise reading and writing in French.

  extra! Activities which provide an extra challenge – have a go!

  ♻️ Activities which give you the chance to recycle language from *Voilà! 1* and *Voilà! 2*.

- The *Sommaire* at the end of each unit lists the key words of the unit in French and English. Use it to look up any words you don't know!

Table des matières *Contents*

1 À Biarritz

1A Estelle et Kévin

- ask and answer questions about name, age, family, etc.
- talk about your hobbies
- say more than the minimum

En août, la famille Cassou arrive à Biarritz. Le 1er septembre, Estelle et Kévin Cassou vont au collège.

Comment t'appelles-tu?

Je m'appelle Estelle.

1 a ♻ 📖 Trouve les paires: questions et réponses.

Exemple: **1 d**

1 Comment t'appelles-tu?

2 Tu as quel âge?

3 Tu habites où?

4 Tu as des frères et sœurs?

5 Tu as un passe-temps?

a J'habite à Biarritz.

b Oui, j'ai un frère. Je n'ai pas de sœur.

c J'ai 14 ans.

d Je m'appelle Estelle.

e Oui, je joue au ping-pong et je fais de la natation.

1 b 💿 Écoute et vérifie.

2 a 📖 Recopie les phrases 1–6. C'est quelle image (A–F)?

Exemple: **1 Je fais du vélo. – F**

1 Je fais du vélo.

2 Je fais de la natation.

3 Je fais du shopping.

4 J'écoute de la musique.

5 Je regarde des DVD.

6 Je joue au ping-pong.

2 b 💿 Écoute les conversations (1–6). C'est quelle image?
extra! Note aussi d'autres détails.

Exemple: **1 C (**extra! **parfois, au collège)**

3 a **Recopie et complète les phrases.**

> écoute   fais (x3)   joue   regarde

Exemple: **1 Je fais du shopping et...**

1 Je ___ du shopping et je ___ au ping-pong.

2 J'___ de la musique et je ___ du vélo.

3 Je ___ de la natation et je ___ des DVD.

3 b **Et toi? Écris la question et *ta* réponse.**

– Tu as un passe-temps?

– Oui, je fais.../je joue.../je regarde.../j'écoute... et je/ j'...

4 ◉ **Écoute et lis le texte. Puis recopie et complète le profil.**

> **Stratégies!** *Giving more information*
>
> When asked what you do in your free time, you'll sound more interesting if you say more than one thing, e.g. *je joue au basket **et** je fais de la danse.*
>
> If you need new words, ask your teacher for help:
> – *Madame/Monsieur, c'est quoi en français,*
>   I go canoeing?
> – *Je fais du canoë.*

Profil
- nom:
- âge:
- ville:
- frère / sœur:
- passe-temps:

> Salut! Je m'appelle Hamed Youssouf. J'ai quinze ans et j'habite à Biarritz. J'ai une sœur, Raïssa, et un frère, Hatim.
>
> Je joue au badminton au centre sportif. Je fais parfois du vélo, et je fais souvent de la natation. En été, je fais du canoë.

5 ◉ **Écoute les questions (1–5). La réponse, c'est a ou b?**

Exemple: **1 b**

1 Je m'appelle   **a** Ali   **b** Florian.

2 **a** Je n'ai pas de sœur.   **b** J'ai un frère et une sœur.

3 J'ai   **a** 13 ans   **b** 15 ans.

4 J'habite à   **a** Lyon   **b** Dijon.

5 Oui,   **a** je joue au basket et je fais du vélo.
       b je joue au foot et je regarde des DVD.

1	comment t'appelles-tu?	je m'appelle *Estelle*
2	tu as quel âge?	j'ai 14 ans
3	tu habites où?	j'habite à *Biarritz*
4	tu as des frères et sœurs?	j'ai un frère et une sœur / je n'ai pas de frère
5	tu as un passe-temps?	je fais du vélo / du shopping / de la natation je joue au ping-pong je regarde des DVD / j'écoute de la musique

6 a **Recopie les questions 1–5 et écris *tes* réponses.**

Exemple: **1 Comment t'appelles-tu? – Je m'appelle...**

6 b 🗨 **Pose les cinq questions à ton/ta partenaire.**

1B La ville et la campagne

- say why you prefer town or country
- write a letter introducing yourself

A les magasins

B la nature

- Tu préfères la campagne...
- Je préfère la campagne.
  - Pourquoi?
  - J'aime... / Je n'aime pas...

... ou la ville?

Je préfère la ville.

C la pollution

D les distractions

entertainments

E le brouhaha

hustle and bustle

F l'odeur de fumier

smell of manure

1 a 💿 Écoute et répète les mots A–F.

1 b 💿 Écoute les conversations (1–6). C'est quelle image (A–F)?
extra! **Note aussi "campagne" ou "ville".**

Exemple: **1 F** (extra! ville)

1 c 🗨 **Joue quatre dialogues différents.**

A Tu préfères la campagne ou la ville?
B Je préfère la campagne.
A Pourquoi?
B J'aime la nature et je n'aime pas le brouhaha.

> ◀ Stratégies! *Giving more detail*
>
> Use the words *mais* (but) and *et* (and)
> to give more than one reason, e.g.
>
> *J'aime la nature **mais** je n'aime pas
> l'odeur de fumier.*

2 ✏ **Écris les phrases.**

Exemple: **1** J'aime le brouhaha...

1 J'aime ▢▢ ▢▢▢▢▢▢▢ mais je n'aime pas ▢▢ ▢▢▢▢▢▢▢.

2 J'aime ▢▢▢ ▢▢▢▢▢▢▢ et j'aime ▢▢▢ ▢▢▢▢▢▢▢▢▢.

3 J'aime ▢▢ ▢▢▢▢▢▢ mais je n'aime pas ▢'▢▢▢▢ ▢▢ ▢▢▢▢▢.

> Nous avons un collège partenaire à York, en Angleterre.
> En mai, on va faire un échange.
> Kévin, ton partenaire s'appelle Sadiq.

> Salut, Sadiq! Je m'appelle Kévin et je suis ton partenaire français. J'habite à Biarritz, dans le sud-ouest de la France. J'ai une sœur jumelle, Estelle.
> J'aime la ville. J'aime les distractions: il y a un centre sportif et une piscine près de ma maison. Je fais du kung-fu au centre sportif.
> Je n'aime pas la campagne. C'est barbant! Et je déteste l'odeur de fumier!
> Et toi, Sadiq? Tu préfères la ville ou la campagne?

une sœur jumelle
– *a twin sister*

Kévin fait une cassette pour Sadiq

3 a 🔘 **Écoute et lis le texte de Kévin. C'est vrai (V) ou faux (F)?**
Exemple: **1 F**

extra! **Corrige les phrases fausses.**
Exemple: **1 F –** *Kévin lives in Biarritz.*

1 *Kévin lives in Paris.*
2 *He has a brother and sister.*
3 *He likes the town.*
4 *He goes to the sports centre.*
5 *He likes the countryside: it's interesting.*
6 *He hates the smell of manure!*

tu préfères la campagne ou la ville?	je préfère…	
pourquoi?		
j'aime… et j'aime…	la nature / l'odeur de fumier / la pollution	
mais je n'aime pas…	les distractions / les magasins / le brouhaha	

3 b 🔘 **Écoute. Il y a une différence? Lève la main.**

4 ✏️ **Écris à Kévin avec:**
  – **des détails personnels** (◀◀ pp. 6–7)
  – **ton opinion sur la ville et la campagne.**

Ton modèle: ▶

- Je m'appelle… et j'habite à…
- J'ai… ans.
- Je joue au… / je fais… / j'écoute… / je regarde…
- Je préfère la ville / la campagne.
- J'aime… et j'aime… Mais je n'aime pas…

1C Le sud-ouest de la France

- say what there is in a region
- pronounce words in the plural
- learn about the south-west of France

J'habite dans le sud-ouest de la France. Dans la région, il y a beaucoup de...

Estelle

A

...collines

B

...plages

Mais il n'y a pas beaucoup de...

C

...villes historiques

D

...lieux de vacances

E

...châteaux

F

...grandes villes

1 a 🗨 Écoute ton/ta prof et répète les phrases A–F:

- il y a beaucoup de...
- il n'y a pas beaucoup de...

Exemple: **(A)** Il y a beaucoup de collines.

1 b 💿 Écoute les deux personnes. Note les lettres A–F dans le bon ordre.

Exemple: **1 C, E, A, ...**

2 a ✏️ Lis les phrases codées. Écris les phrases en français!

1 Il y ✳ be✳ucoup de pl✳ges.
2 Il y ✳ be✳ucoup de châte✳ux.
3 Il y ✳ be✳ucoup de gr✳ndes v❤lles.
4 Il n'y ✳ p✳s be✳ucoup de l❤eux de v✳c✳nces.
5 Il n'y ✳ p✳s be✳ucoup de v❤lles h❤stor❤ques.
6 Il n'y ✳ p✳s be✳ucoup de coll❤nes.

Le symbole ✳ = la lettre 💡
Le symbole ❤ = la lettre 💡

2 b ✏️ extra! Écris quatre phrases codées pour ton/ta partenaire. Ton/Ta partenaire écrit les phrases en français.

3 a 💿 Écoute (1–6) et regarde la carte. C'est vrai (V) ou faux (F)?

Exemple: **1 V**

> **Grammaire:** plurals
>
> Most plural nouns and adjectives end in **-s**,
> e.g. ville**s** historique**s**
> but note this exception: château**x**.
>
> Remember not to pronounce the -s and -x when speaking.

3 b 💬 Quiz! C'est quelle région?

Exemple: **A** Il y a beaucoup de châteaux.
B C'est la Dordogne.

3 c ✏️ Regarde la carte. Écris six phrases.

Exemple: **En Vendée, il y a beaucoup de plages.**

j'habite dans le sud-ouest de la France	
dans la région il y a beaucoup de…	collines / villes historiques / grandes villes
il n'y a pas beaucoup de…	plages / châteaux / lieux de vacances

(Map of France with regions labelled: la Normandie, la Lorraine, la Vendée, l'Auvergne, la Provence, la Dordogne)

4 a 📖 Read Estelle's text and note three facts in English about south-west France.

Le sud-ouest de la France est près de l'Espagne. Il y a beaucoup de collines et de montagnes et beaucoup de villes historiques. Il n'y a pas beaucoup de grandes villes, et pas beaucoup de pollution.

Il y a beaucoup de plages, c'est génial: j'aime la natation!

Estelle

Les Pyrénées en été

4 b 📖 extra! Read Fabien's text, and note three facts in English.

Les trois "grands" sports du sud-ouest de la France sont le rugby, le surf et la pelote. La pelote, c'est un jeu basque.

Biarritz est la capitale européenne du surf. Il y a un festival international de surf en juillet.

Fabien

La pelote, un jeu basque

1D Une cassette pour la France

- give a short presentation
- use the right word for 'in': à or dans
- use the Sommaire to look up words

Stratégies! ***Recording a message***

You are going to send a cassette about yourself to a French pen-friend.

- Study an example (exercise 1).
- Adapt the sentences to apply to yourself (exercises 2 & 3).
- Record your cassette (exercise 4).

1 Je m'appelle Sadiq et j'ai quatorze ans. J'ai un frère et une sœur. Je joue au tennis.

2 J'habite à York dans le nord de l'Angleterre. Dans la région il y a beaucoup de villes historiques, mais près de York il n'y a pas beaucoup de collines.

3 J'aime la ville. J'aime les distractions, mais je n'aime pas la pollution.

1 💿 **Écoute et lis. C'est le paragraphe 1, 2 ou 3?**
Sadiq mentionne...

1	son nom	**4**	sa région
2	son opinion sur York	**5**	sa famille
3	son âge	**6**	un passe-temps

Grammaire: two words for 'in': *à* + town, *dans* + the south, west, etc.

j'habite **à** *Carlisle* **dans...**

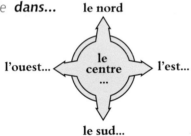

le nord

l'ouest...   le centre ...   l'est...

le sud...

de l'Angleterre
de l'Écosse
du pays de Galles
de l'Irlande du Nord

2 ***Write and learn a sentence which applies to you!***

3 🖋 **Change les mots en rouge et écris *tes détails*.**

Exemple: **1 Je m'appelle *Michael* et j'ai *quatorze* ans.**

1   Je m'appelle Rachel et j'ai quinze ans.
2   J'ai deux frères et je n'ai pas de sœur.
3   J'écoute de la musique et je fais de la natation.
4   J'habite à St Andrews dans l'est de l'Écosse.
5   Dans la région il y a beaucoup de plages, mais il n'y a pas beaucoup de grandes villes.
6   J'aime la ville. J'aime les distractions.

◄ Stratégies! **Getting help**

Look at the *Sommaire* on page 13 to remind you of words you might need.

4 **À toi! Fais ta cassette pour ton/ta partenaire en France (5–6 phrases).**

extra! **7–8 phrases!**

Estelle et Kévin	Estelle and Kévin
comment t'appelles-tu?	what's your name?
je m'appelle Estelle	my name is Estelle
tu as quel âge?	how old are you?
j'ai quatorze ans	I'm 14 years old
tu habites où?	where do you live?
j'habite à Biarritz	I live in Biarritz
tu as des frères et sœurs?	do you have any brothers and sisters?
j'ai un frère et une sœur	I have brother and a sister
je n'ai pas de frère	I don't have a brother
tu as un passe-temps?	do you have a hobby?
je fais du vélo	I go cycling
je fais du shopping	I go shopping
je fais de la natation	I go swimming
je joue au ping-pong	I play table-tennis
je regarde des DVD	I watch DVDs
j'écoute de la musique	I listen to music

La ville et la campagne	Town and countryside
tu préfères la campagne ou la ville?	do you prefer the countryside or the town?
je préfère...	I prefer...
pourquoi?	why?
j'aime...	I like...
mais je n'aime pas...	but I don't like...
le brouhaha	the hustle and bustle
la nature	nature
la pollution	pollution
l'odeur de fumier	the smell of manure
les distractions	the entertainments
les magasins	the shops

Le sud-ouest	The south-west
j'habite dans le sud-ouest de la France	I live in the south-west of France
dans la région	in the region
il y a beaucoup de...	there are a lot of...
il n'y a pas beaucoup de...	there aren't a lot of...
collines	hills
villes historiques	historic towns
grandes villes	big towns/cities
plages	beaches
châteaux	castles
lieux de vacances	holiday resorts

Grammaire

● plurals:
  – most plural nouns and adjectives end in –**s**: ville**s** historique**s**
  – note the exception: château**x**
  – remember not to pronounce the -**s** and -**x** when speaking
● two words for 'in':
  – **à** + town   j'habite à Carlisle / j'habite à Biarritz
  – **dans** + point of the compass   dans le sud / dans le nord

Stratégies!

★ giving more information: asking your teacher for new words; using *et* and *mais*

★ recording a message: study an example, adapt the sentences to apply to yourself, record your cassette; use the *Sommaire* for reference

2 meanings
je **fais** mes devoirs – I **do** my homework
je **fais** du vélo – I **go** cycling

2 La télé et la musique

2A À la télé

- discuss different sorts of TV programme
- use knowledge of French word order to understand new words

Une vidéoconférence...

Sadiq (en Angleterre) parle à Kévin (en France).

Je n'aime pas les séries comme *EastEnders*. Mais j'aime les émissions de sport.

---

1 a Grammaire: word order

In French phrases, words are sometimes in the reverse order from English.

Can you work out phrases B–E?
e.g. *les émissions de sport* – sports programmes

1 b 💿 Écoute Sadiq. Il aime ☺ ou il n'aime pas ☹ les émissions A–H?

Exemple: **A** ☹

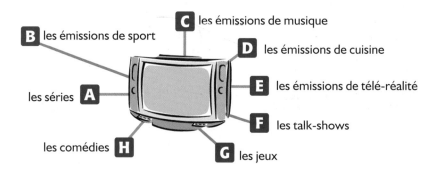

B les émissions de sport
C les émissions de musique
D les émissions de cuisine
les séries **A**
E les émissions de télé-réalité
F les talk-shows
les comédies **H**
G les jeux

1 c ✏️ Écris une phrase pour chaque image (1–6).

Exemple: **1** J'aime les séries.
2 Je n'aime pas...

2 💬 Pose six questions à ton/ta partenaire.

Exemple: **A** J'adore les émissions de sport comme *Grandstand*. Et toi?
B Moi aussi./Moi, non.

3 Écoute et note le pourcentage de personnes qui ont le satellite/le câble:

a en Belgique   **b** en Grande-Bretagne   **c** en Scandinavie   **d** en Allemagne

33%

10%   80%

80%

4 Lis les trois textes.

1 Qui aime **a** les émissions de musique   **b** les émissions de télé-réalité?

2 L'opinion de Mohamed sur *Inspecteur Derrick*: c'est Super! ou OK, mais... ?

3 *Loft Story*, c'est une émission de cuisine ou une émission de télé-réalité?

> J'aime les émissions de sport, et j'adore les émissions de musique comme *MTV Select*.
> Chloé

> Je n'aime pas les séries comme *Dawson*. *Dawson*, c'est barbant! Mais *Inspecteur Derrick* est assez bien.
> Mohamed

> Moi, j'aime les émissions de cuisine et j'adore les émissions de télé-réalité comme *Loft Story*. Ça, c'est très amusant!
> Fabien

5 a Écoute (1–8) et regarde le diagramme. On mentionne quels types d'émission?

Exemple: **1 les jeux + les séries**

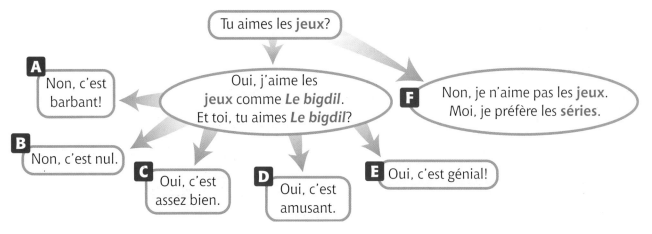

5 b Réécoute. La conversation finit où dans le diagramme (A–F)?

Exemple: **1 F**

5 c Regarde le diagramme et joue six conversations.

6 Écris quatre phrases sur la télé.

extra! Écris huit phrases.

Exemple: **J'aime les séries comme** *Casualty*: *Casualty*, c'est génial.

tu aimes... ?	j'aime...	j'adore...	je n'aime pas...
les jeux / les talk-shows / les séries / les comédies			
les émissions de cuisine / de sport / de musique / de télé-réalité			
j'aime les séries comme *Casualty*			
c'est	assez bien / amusant / nul / barbant		
moi aussi	moi, non	je préfère les séries	

2B Opinions sur la télé

- exchange views about TV
- use phrases with *de*
- say long sentences
- give a presentation

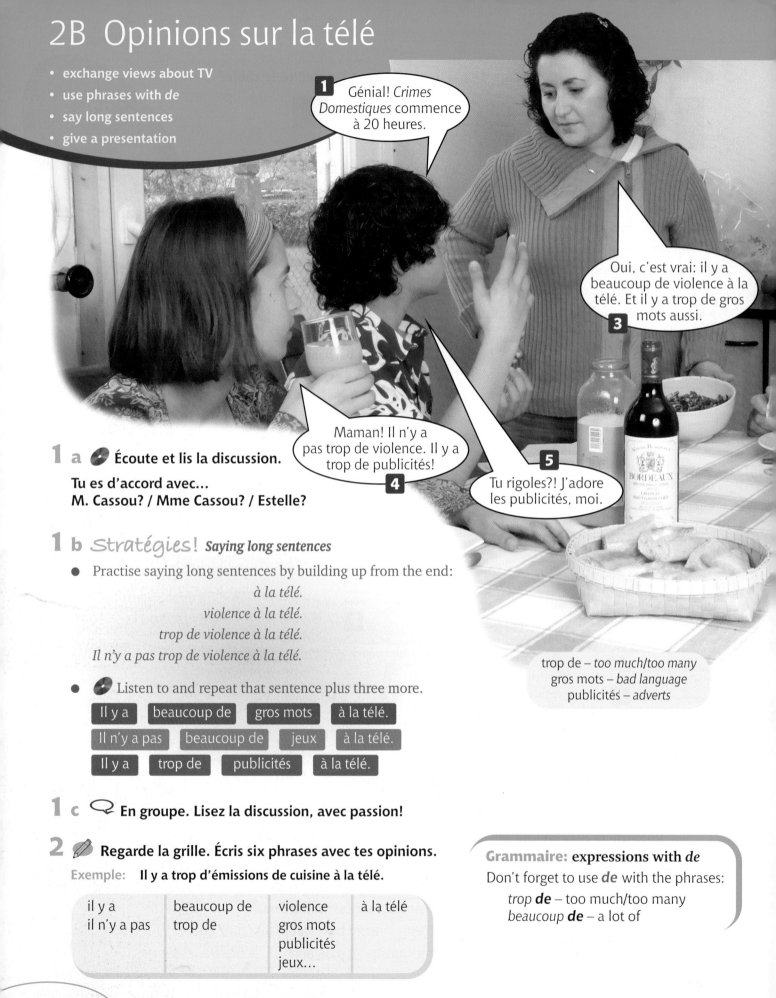

1 Génial! *Crimes Domestiques* commence à 20 heures.

3 Oui, c'est vrai: il y a beaucoup de violence à la télé. Et il y a trop de gros mots aussi.

4 Maman! Il n'y a pas trop de violence. Il y a trop de publicités!

5 Tu rigoles?! J'adore les publicités, moi.

1 a 🔊 **Écoute et lis la discussion.**

Tu es d'accord avec…
M. Cassou? / Mme Cassou? / Estelle?

1 b Stratégies! *Saying long sentences*

- Practise saying long sentences by building up from the end:

  à la télé.
  violence à la télé.
  trop de violence à la télé.
  Il n'y a pas trop de violence à la télé.

- 💿 Listen to and repeat that sentence plus three more.

Il y a	beaucoup de	gros mots	à la télé.
Il n'y a pas	beaucoup de	jeux	à la télé.
Il y a	trop de	publicités	à la télé.

1 c 💬 **En groupe. Lisez la discussion, avec passion!**

2 ✏️ **Regarde la grille. Écris six phrases avec tes opinions.**

Exemple: **Il y a trop d'émissions de cuisine à la télé.**

| il y a
il n'y a pas | beaucoup de
trop de | violence
gros mots
publicités
jeux… | à la télé |

trop de – too much/too many
gros mots – bad language
publicités – adverts

Grammaire: expressions with *de*
Don't forget to use **de** with the phrases:
*trop **de** – too much/too many*
*beaucoup **de** – a lot of*

2 Non, pas pour toi, Kévin. Il y a trop de violence.

3 💬 **Discute de tes opinions.**

Exemple: **A** Il y a trop de jeux à la télé.
  B Oui, c'est vrai.
  ou
  Tu rigoles!

> c'est vrai *that's true*
> tu rigoles! *you're joking!*

4a 💿 **Sophie parle de la télé. Écoute et lis. C'est vrai (V) ou faux (F)?**

Exemple: **1 F**

1 Sophie n'aime pas la télé.
2 Elle adore les comédies.
3 *La Ferme* est une émission de musique.
4 Sophie aime les publicités.
5 Son opinion: il y a trop de sport à la télé.
6 Son opinion: il n'y a pas trop de violence à la télé.

> Moi, j'aime beaucoup la télé. J'adore les séries et les comédies. J'aime les émissions de télé-réalité, comme *La Ferme*. Ça, c'est amusant.
>
> Moi, personnellement, je déteste les publicités. Je n'aime pas les émissions de sport, comme *Téléfoot*. C'est vraiment barbant. À mon avis, il y a trop d'émissions de sport à la télé. Et il y a trop de violence, aussi.

4b 💿 **Écoute. Il y a une différence? Lève la main.**

5 Stratégies! *Giving a presentation*

Your task: to present your views about television.

Step 1   Use Sophie's presentation as a model. Make notes on your opinions using words from this section and from section A.

  Example: *J'aime les séries comme* Casualty.

Step 2   extra! Pick out and use any other useful words from Sophie's presentation.

  Example: *à mon avis* – in my opinion
  À mon avis, il y a trop de violence.

Step 3   Ask your partner to check your notes. Then write out your corrected sentences as a full text.

Step 4   Read your presentation aloud, to practise your pronunciation.

  ● Read it to your partner.
  ● Record yourself and listen. How can you sound more French?

OK? Give your presentation.

2C On regarde la télé?

- understand a TV listing
- look for clues in a longer text
- discuss what to watch

1 a Stratégies!

Class shared reading: looking for clues

The TV programme listing on page 19 is quite long but you don't need to understand every word (e.g. the plot of the films).

- How does the layout help you to spot the times of the programmes, their names and the type of programme?

1 b 📖 Lis le guide à la page 19.

Recopie le nom...

1 d'une série	**5** d'une émission de musique
2 d'un jeu	**6** d'une émission de cuisine
3 d'un film	**7** d'une émission de sport
4 d'un talk-show	**8** d'une émission de télé-réalité.

il est	dix-sept heures	cinq
		quinze
		vingt
		trente-cinq
		quarante
		cinquante

2 a ♻ Regarde les photos 1–6. Quelle heure est-il?

Exemple: **1 Il est dix-sept heures trente-cinq.**

2 b 💿 Regarde le guide et écoute (1–6).

L'heure de l'émission, c'est vrai (V) ou faux (F)?

Exemple: **1 V**

1 *Dawson*
2 *Sous le soleil*
3 *Fête de la musique*
4 *Cruelles intentions*
5 *le Football*
6 *C'est mon choix*

3 💿 Écoute les deux dialogues. Puis discute de six émissions avec ton/ta partenaire.

A Tu veux regarder *Fête de la musique*?
B C'est à quelle heure?
A À 17 heures 55, sur France 2.
B OK. J'aime les émissions de musique.

A Tu veux regarder *Dawson*?
B C'est à quelle heure?
A À 16 heures 45, sur TF1.
B Non, je n'aime pas les séries.

tu veux regarder...?
c'est à quelle heure?
à *17h55*, sur *France 2*
OK, j'aime les *séries* / non, je n'aime pas les *séries*

16.45 Dawson

Série américaine. Pacey revient au lycée après une semaine d'exclusion...

18.00 Le bigdil

Jeu. Avec Vincent Lagaf'.

18.50 Sous le soleil

Série française. Aurélie a préparé son mariage et décide de l'annoncer à son père. Maxime est furieux.

19.50 Qui veut gagner des millions?

Jeu. Avec Jean-Pierre Foucault.

20.50 La ferme célébrités

Télé-réalité. Six femmes et six hommes célèbres sont entrés dans une ferme du Haut-Var, au nord de Toulon. Ces VIP doivent vivre pendant 13 semaines sans eau et sans électricité.

16.50 Inspecteur Derrick

Série culte. Le corps d'un homme battu à mort a été trouvé dans un parc. On sollicite l'inspecteur Derrick...

17.55 Fête de la musique

Le rappeur populaire MC Solaar, des stars canadiennes, anglaises et brésiliennes: embarquez pour la nuit la plus chaude de l'année!

19.05 Cruelles intentions

Film. Comédie dramatique de Roger Kumble. USA 2000. Avec Robin Dunne, Sarah Thompson.

Dans un collège de New York, Sébastien, passé maître dans l'art de la séduction, fait la connaissance de Kathryn...

17.00 Bon appétit, bien sûr

Salade de fruits tropicaux, préparée par le chef Catherine Guerraz.

17.30 Football: Bordeaux/Sochaux

Ligue 1. En direct.

19.30 C'est mon choix

Talk show, animé par Evelyne Thomas

20.15 Fabio Montale: Chourmo

Film policier de José Pinhiero. France 2001. Avec Alain Delon, Cédric Chevalme, Laure Killing, Mathilda May.

Peu avant sa retraite, Fabio Montale reçoit la visite de sa cousine, Angie. Inquiète, elle lui demande d'enquêter sur la disparition de son fils de 16 ans.

2D La musique française

Alizée (1984–)

Alizée, révélation française aux M6 Awards et NRJ Music Awards, a chanté en Europe, au Canada, en Russie et au Japon.

Georges Bizet (1838–1875)

Compositeur du célèbre opéra *Carmen*.

Maurice Ravel 1875–1937)

Compositeur de musique classique pour piano, violon, et orchestre, par exemple le célèbre "Boléro".

Édith Piaf (1915–1963)

Chanteuse légendaire des années 30, 40 et 50.

1 a 📖 Lis les quatre textes. Écris les noms dans l'ordre chronologique.

1 b 💿 Écoute la musique et identifie les deux musiciens.

2 a 💿 Écoute et lis le rap. *What is the effect of TV in the singer's family?*

Example:
The singer doesn't speak to...

2 b ✏️ Recopie en français:

a **1** *type of drink*

b **2** *types of TV programme*

c **3** *members of the family*

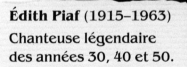

La télé-réalité

Je ne parle pas à ma mère:
Elle est dans le salon.
Elle ignore mon p'tit frère
Et regarde la télévision.

*Les émissions
de télévision –
c'est la fin
de la communication!*

Je ne parle pas à mon père:
Il regarde la télé.
Un fauteuil et une bière,
C'est sa télé-réalité.

Je ne parle pas à mon frère:
Je regarde une série.
Je ne veux rien faire
Avec ma famille.

Sommaire

À la télé	On TV
tu aimes... ?	*do you like... ?*
j'aime...	*I like...*
j'adore...	*I love...*
je n'aime pas...	*I don't like...*
les jeux *m*	*game shows*
les talk-shows *m*	*talk shows*
les séries *f*	*series/soaps*
les comédies *f*	*comedies*
les émissions *f*	
de cuisine	*cookery programmes*
de sport	*sports programmes*
de musique	*music programmes*
de télé-réalité	*reality TV shows*
moi aussi	*me too*
moi, non	*I don't*
je préfère...	*I prefer...*
j'aime les séries comme	*I like series like*
Casualty	*Casualty*
c'est...	*it's...*
assez bien	*quite good*
amusant	*fun / funny*
nul	*rubbish*
barbant	*boring*

Opinions sur la télé	Opinions about TV
il y a beaucoup de...	*there's a lot of...*
il n'y a pas beaucoup de...	*there isn't a lot of...*
il y a trop de...	*there's too much/there are too many...*
il n'y a pas trop de...	*there isn't too much/there aren't too many...*
violence	*violence*
gros mots	*bad language*
publicités	*adverts*
à la télé	*on TV*
c'est vrai	*that's true*
tu rigoles!	*you're joking!*

On regarde la télé?	Shall we watch TV?
il est dix-sept heures...	*it's...*
cinq	*17.05*
quinze	*17.15*
vingt	*17.20*
trente-cinq	*17.35*
quarante	*17.40*
cinquante	*17.50*
tu veux regarder *Le bigdil*?	*do you want to watch Le bigdil?*
c'est à quelle heure?	*what time is it on?*
à 17h55	*at 17.55*
sur France 2	*on France 2*
OK, j'aime les jeux	*OK, I like game shows*
non, je n'aime pas les jeux	*no, I don't like game shows*

Grammaire

- French word order is often the reverse of English: *télé-réalité* – reality TV
- use **de** with the phrases: *beaucoup de* a lot of, *trop de* too much/too many

Stratégies!

★ practising saying long sentences by building up from the end

★ giving a presentation

★ looking for clues in a longer text: using layout to help

une émission de **cuisine** – a **cookery** programme
la **cuisine** – the **kitchen**

Stratégies! *Preparing for your assessment*

- Look back at the *Sommaire* pages for unit 1 (p. 13) and unit 2 (p. 21) and check to see which words you can remember. (This is much easier with a partner.)

- Then focus on the ones you *can't* remember:
  - Write out up to ten words or phrases you can't remember.
  - Ask your partner to test you *on these words only*.

1 a ✏ Écris les mots du dialogue dans le bon ordre.

1 b 💬 Joue le dialogue.

1 c 💬 Adapte le dialogue: donne *tes* réponses.

Stratégies! *Giving more information*

Remember to mention more than one hobby:
*Je joue au foot **et** je regarde...*

- Comment -tu? t'appelles
- m'appelle Aurélie Je
- quel Tu âge? as
- ans J'ai quatorze
- frères des et Tu sœurs? as
- sœur frère et J'ai un une
- Tu passe-temps? un as
- fais je Oui, vélo du
- Tu talk-shows? les aimes
- j'aime de sport les Non, émissions

2 💿 Écoute (1–6). Note ✓ (= il y a) ou ✗ (= il n'y a pas).

Exemple: 1 ✗

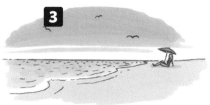

3 📖 Lis le texte et réponds aux questions en anglais.

1 *Where does Monsieur Gilbert live?*
2 *Which of the following does he **not** like?*
   a *shops*
   b *reality TV programmes*
   c *cookery programmes*
   d *the hustle and bustle in town*
3 *What is his ambition?*

Monsieur Gilbert

Monsieur Gilbert est prof de maths. Il habite dans le sud de la Belgique. M. Gilbert n'aime pas son collège, il n'aime pas le brouhaha de la ville, et il n'aime pas les magasins.

Mais il aime la télé: il adore les émissions de télé-réalité et de cuisine!

Et il a une ambition: il veut participer à une émission de télé-réalité.

La Nouvelle Star

Le 27 mars, la chaîne de télé M6 a commencé le grand casting pour l'émission de musique: *À la recherche de la nouvelle star.*

20 000 personnes ont chanté devant le jury de M6! Les auditions, le vote du public, etc., c'est comme *Pop Idol* en Grande-Bretagne. Mais l'heure de l'émission est différente: le "prime time" en France commence à 20h50; en Angleterre, *Pop Idol* passe à 19h30.

Mon audition:

8 heures d'attente...

9h: j'arrive. Les premiers candidats sont arrivés à 7h.

Un candidat s'appelle Thomas.

"Tu chantes souvent en public?" demande Thomas.

"Non, jamais," je réponds.

"Ah?" dit Thomas. "*Moi*, je chante souvent!"

... 5 minutes d'audition

Après huit heures de queue, j'arrive devant le jury.

Les deux personnes du jury sont sympas. Je chante ma chanson... mais je ne chante pas bien.

Et je ne suis pas sélectionnée.

Lucie

© OKAPI, Bayard Jeunesse, 2003

a commencé – *started*
ont chanté – *sang*
passe à – *is on at*
attente – *waiting*
devant – *in front of*

C'est moi, Lucie, la nouvelle star

Huit heures d'attente...

---

1 **Read the article and answer the questions.**

  1 *What sort of TV programme is this article about?*

  2 *In what ways are the British and French versions of the programme **a** similar **b** different?*

  3 *Is Lucie used to singing in public?*

  4 *How long does she have to queue for?*

  5 *Is Lucie selected for the next round?*

  6 extra! *What's the name of the French equivalent of Pop Idol? What does the name mean in English? (You can look the words up in the Glossaire, pp.133–141.)*

3 La semaine dernière

3A Au parc d'attractions

- describe a trip to a theme park
- use the past tense
- meet the French names for rides

Samedi dernier, Estelle et Kévin sont allés dans un parc d'attractions.

J'ai fait un tour **A** sur le roller coaster. C'était hilarant!

Après ça, j'ai fait un tour sur la grande roue. C'était assez bien. **B**

> j'ai fait un tour sur... – *I went on...*

D Après ça, j'ai fait un tour sur le bateau renverseur. C'était terrifiant – et génial!

BARBE A PAPA 2€

C

J'ai acheté de la barbe à papa. Miam-miam! J'adore ça!

E

JUS D'ORANGE

Puis, j'ai acheté un jus d'orange...

et un hot-dog.

1 a 💿 Écoute (1–2). Écris les lettres A–E dans le bon ordre.

Exemple: **1** C, ...

1 b ✏️ Écris six phrases en français et en anglais.

Exemple: J'ai fait un tour sur la grande roue. – *I went on the big wheel.*

J'ai fait un tour sur...	la grande roue	un jus d'orange
J'ai acheté...	assez bien	terrifiant
C'était...	un hot-dog	le roller coaster

2 a 🔘 Regarde les images. Écoute (1–8).
Note l'opinion sur le tour:

🙂 , 😐 ou 🙁 .

Exemple: **1** 🙂

♻️ **Grammaire:** *le passé* **the past tense**

present	past	Note:
je fais	j'ai fait	**j'ai** (not *je*) in the past.
j'achète	j'ai acheté	the -**é** ending in the past *is* pronounced; it isn't optional!
c'est	c'était	c'est = it is c'était = it was

Les attractions du parc

les autos tamponneuses

le roller coaster

le bateau renverseur

les karts

les rapides

la grande roue

2 b 💬 Joue les deux dialogues.
extra! Invente un troisième dialogue!

1

A Tu as fait un tour sur ?

B Non, j'ai fait un tour sur

A C'était bien?

B Oui, c'était 🙂.

A Tu as acheté un ?

B Non, j'ai acheté des frites..

2

B Tu as...

A Non, j'ai...

B C'était bien?

A Non, c'était 🙁.

A Tu as... ?

B Non, j'ai acheté un coca.

3 ✏️ Imagine une visite au parc d'attractions. Écris 6–8 phrases.

Au parc d'attractions, j'ai...

j'ai fait	un tour sur	*le roller coaster*
j'ai acheté	un hot-dog / un jus d'orange	
c'était	hilarant / terrifiant / assez bien / génial / nul	

3B La boutique du parc

- prices, and buying things at a gift shop
- use the right words for 'this' and 'these'
- understand a French advert

Stratégies! *Tricky numbers*

- If the next word begins with a vowel (e.g. *euros*) 2 *deux*, 10 *dix* and 12 *douze* all end in a **z** sound. So for example *deux euros* sounds like "*deuzzeuro*".

- This table may help you with these numbers:

4 *quatre*	14 *quatorze*	40 *quarante*
5 *cinq*	15 *quinze*	50 *cinquante*
6 *six*	16 *seize*	60 *soixante*

1 a 💿 **Écoute les prix (1–5). C'est a, b ou c?** ◀

1 a 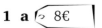 8€ b 18€ c 28€

2 a 4€ b 14€ c 40€

3 a 6€ b 16€ c 60€

4 a 2€ b 10€ c 12€

5 a 5,40€ b 5,50€ c 5,60€

1 b 💿 **Écoute (1–6) et note les prix.**

2 a 💿 **Écoute les conversations 1–8 et regarde les photos. Les prix sont corrects: oui ou non?**

C'est combien... ?

 6,90€

4,50€

ce porte-monnaie	ce bloc-notes
cette carte postale	cette bague

 19,50€

 9,90€

cet appareil-photo	cet album de photos
ces bics	ces bonbons

 0,50€

 6,60€

 1,99€

 1,25€

2 b 💬 **A demande le prix; B dit le prix.**

Exemple:
A C'est combien, ces bics?
B Un euro quatre-vingt-dix-neuf.

2 c ✏️ **Anagrammes: écris les mots.**

Exemple: **1 ce bloc-notes**

1 ce **CLOB-TONES**

2 cette **CRATE SPATOLE**

3 cet **BALUM de THOSOP**

4 ces **CIBS**

5 ces **SNOBBON**

6 ce **TROPE-NANIOME**

7 cet **ARLEPIPA-POTHO**

8 cette **GABUE**

Grammaire: *ce, cet, cette* (this), *ces* (these)

masculine singular nouns	feminine singular nouns	all plural nouns
ce bloc-notes this pad	*cette* bague this ring	*ces* bics these biros
*cet appareil-photo this camera		

* use *cet* with masculine singular nouns that begin with a vowel or *h*.

3 **Écris une question pour les images 1–5. (*extra!* 1–8)**

Exemple: **1 C'est combien, ces bonbons?**

  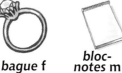

| **bonbons** pl | **bague** f | **bloc-notes** m | **bics** pl | **casquette** f | **T-shirt** m | **pommes** pl | **CD** m |

4 a **Écoute et lis. Puis joue le dialogue.**

– Pardon, monsieur. C'est combien, cet album de photos?
– C'est dix euros cinquante.
– C'est bon.
– C'est tout, madame?
– Oui, c'est tout.
– Alors, dix euros cinquante, madame.
– Voilà. Merci, monsieur. Au revoir.

4 b  **Invente quatre dialogues similaires.**

Adopte un caractère, par exemple impatient, enthousiaste, terrifiant, …

pardon, monsieur/madame c'est combien, cette bague?	c'est… euros. voilà. c'est tout?
oui, c'est tout	alors, dix euros cinquante
voilà. merci. au revoir	

4 c  **Écris un dialogue.**

5  **Class shared reading.**
Read this camera advert from a French website. Can you find out:
1 *the original price*
2 *how much you save*
3 *the offer price*
4 *the length of the guarantee?*

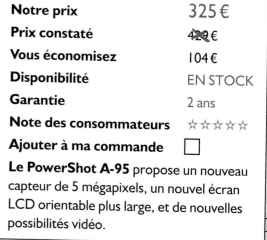

Canon Powershot A95

Notre prix	325 €
Prix constaté	429 €
Vous économisez	104 €
Disponibilité	EN STOCK
Garantie	2 ans
Note des consommateurs	☆☆☆☆☆
Ajouter à ma commande	☐

Zoomer

Envoyer à un ami

Le PowerShot A-95 propose un nouveau capteur de 5 mégapixels, un nouvel écran LCD orientable plus large, et de nouvelles possibilités vidéo.

3C Un samedi désastreux

- describe a day when everything went wrong
- use the past tense
- look up words in the glossary

Samedi, c'était un désastre!

A *Le matin, j'ai téléphoné à un copain, Noé,...*

... mais il **n'était pas là.**

n'était pas là – wasn't there

B *Après ça, j'ai tchatché sur Internet...*

...c'était stupide!

C *À midi, ma sœur et moi, on a joué au tennis...*

... mais il faisait mauvais!

il faisait mauvais – the weather was bad

D *Le soir, on a mangé une pizza...*

... mais c'était horrible!

E *Après ça, on a regardé un film...*

... mais c'était barbant!

1 a 💿 Écoute et lis A–E.

1 b 💿 Réécoute. Il y a une différence? Lève la main.

1 c Stratégies! *Time expressions*

Time expressions (e.g. *le matin* – in the morning), make a text 'flow' better.

- Find four time expressions in A–E above.
- Write them in French and English. If necessary, look them up in the *Glossaire* (pp. 133–141).

le matin,	j'ai	téléphoné à *un copain*
à midi,	on a	mangé *une pizza*
après ça,		regardé *un film*
le soir,		tchatché sur Internet
		joué au *tennis*
c'était	nul / stupide / horrible / barbant	
il faisait mauvais		

Grammaire: *le passé* the past tense

- *j'ai —é* = what **I** did   *j'ai mangé* I ate
- *on a —é* = what **we** did   *on a mangé* we ate

1 d 📖 Écris les verbes en français et en anglais pour les images A–E.

Exemple: **A** j'ai téléphoné – *I phoned*

I	chatted	ate	watched
we		played	phoned

2 ♻️ 🖋️ Recopie les expressions possibles.

Exemple: **J'ai regardé un film, une…**

1 J'ai regardé `un film` `une émission de musique` `la géographie` `un match de foot`

2 J'ai téléphoné à `un chien` `un ami` `mon cousin` `ma mère` `une copine`

3 On a tchatché sur Internet, et c'était `super` `grand` `stupide` `nul` `assez bien`

4 On a mangé `du poisson` `des biscuits` `des pommes` `mon copain`

5 Il faisait `mauvais` `beau` `petite` `froid`

3 a 📖 **Lis les descriptions de problèmes (1–3) et regarde les images (A–C). Trouve les paires.**

Stratégies! **Using the glossary**

- Check unknown words in the *Glossaire*.
- Verbs are listed in the infinitive, so for *j'ai ajouté* look up *ajouter*.

1 J'ai fait un gateau au chocolat. Miam-miam? Non! J'ai ajouté du sel, pas du sucre!
Martin

2 Le soir, j'ai eu trois heures de devoirs de maths et deux heures de devoirs de français!
Hamed

3 Je suis allé au parc avec ma petite sœur (elle a trois ans). J'ai bavardé avec une copine. Mais après, ma petite sœur n'était pas là!
Anthony

3 b 📖 *Explain the problems in English.*

4 🖋️ extra! **Invente une série de problèmes: adapte quatre phrases de l'exercice 1 ou 3.**

Exemple: **J'ai téléphoné à *une copine*, *Claire*, mais *elle* n'était pas là.**

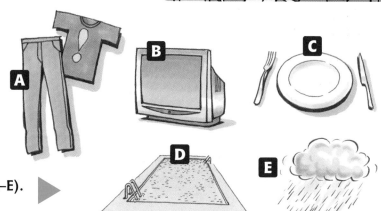

5 ♻️ 🎧 **Écoute (1–5). Identifie le thème (A–E).**

Exemple: **1 B**

3D Une excursion de classe

- describe a class trip in the past
- build up a description in a sequence of short steps

> Jeudi, on a fait une excursion à Carcassonne. Thomas a vomi dans le car. Berk! C'était horrible.
>
> Le matin, on a visité la ville avec un guide intéressant et amusant.
>
> À midi, on a fait un pique-nique et j'ai acheté un coca.
>
> Après ça, on a joué au foot. Mais j'ai perdu mon appareil-photo.
>
> L'excursion, c'était génial, à part le désastre de mon appareil-photo!

le car – *coach*
on a eu – *we had*

1 💿 **Écoute et lis. Après ça, recopie une expression pour chaque image (A–F).**

Exemple: **A** Après ça, on a joué au foot.

Carcassonne, ville historique

2 a 💿 **Écoute deux conversations. Note les bonnes lettres (A–J).**

Exemple: **1** B, D, …

– Jeudi, on a fait une excursion à **A** Ironbridge. **B** Alnwick.
  Le matin, on a visité **C** le musée. **D** le château.
– Et à midi?
– À midi, **E** on a fait un pique-nique. **F** Jason a vomi dans le café.
– Et après ça ?
– Après ça, **G** on a joué au volley dans le parc. **H** j'ai perdu mon porte-monnaie.
– L'excursion, c'était bien?
– **I** Oui, c'était génial! **J** Non, c'était nul.

2 b 💬 **Joue deux dialogues.**

3 ✏️ extra! **Décris une excursion. Invente les détails.**

Exemple: *Mardi*, on a fait une excursion...

Stratégies! *Describing a day out*

It's easier if you think of the trip as five steps:
1 where you went
2 what you did in the morning
3 lunch
4 what you did in the afternoon
5 a final comment

Write one sentence for each step.

jeudi, on a fait une excursion à *Warwick*	
le matin,	*Jason* a vomi dans *le car*
à midi,	on a visité *la ville* / on a joué au foot
après ça,	on a fait un pique-nique
	j'ai acheté *un coca*
	j'ai perdu *mon appareil-photo*
l'excursion, c'était	génial / amusant / nul

Au parc d'attractions / At the theme park

j'ai fait un tour sur le roller coaster	I went on the roller coaster
j'ai acheté...	I bought...
un hot-dog	a hot dog
un jus d'orange	an orange juice
c'était...	it was...
hilarant	hilarious
terrifiant	terrifying
génial	great
assez bien	quite good
nul	rubbish

La boutique / The shop

c'est combien... ?	how much is/are... ?
ce porte-monnaie	this purse
ce bloc-notes	this notepad
cet appareil-photo	this camera
cet album de photos	this photo album
cette carte postale	this postcard
cette bague	this ring
ces bics	these biros
ces bonbons	these sweets
pardon, monsieur	excuse me (to a man)
pardon, madame	excuse me (to a woman)
c'est... euros	it's... euros
voilà	here you are
c'est tout?	is that all?
oui, c'est tout	yes, that's everything
alors, dix euros cinquante	so, that's 10,50€
merci	thank you
au revoir	goodbye

Un samedi désastreux / A disastrous Saturday

le matin	in the morning
à midi	at midday
après ça	after that
le soir	in the evening
j'ai téléphoné à un copain	I phoned a friend (male)
j'ai mangé une pizza	I ate a pizza
j'ai tchatché sur Internet	I chatted on the Internet
on a regardé un film	we watched a film
on a joué au tennis	we played tennis
c'était...	it was...
nul	rubbish
stupide	stupid
horrible	horrible
barbant	boring
il faisait mauvais	the weather was bad

Une excursion / A trip

jeudi, on a fait une excursion à Warwick	on Thursday we went on a trip to Warwick
il a vomi dans le car	he was sick in the coach
on a visité la ville	we visited the town
on a joué au foot	we played football
on a fait un pique-nique	we had a picnic
j'ai acheté un coca	I bought a coke
j'ai perdu mon appareil-photo	I lost my camera
l'excursion, c'était...	the trip was...
amusant	fun
génial	great

Grammaire

- **le passé** the past tense

I	j'ai	acheté, mangé, visité, joué,
we	on a	regardé, fait, vomi, perdu, etc.

- **this, these**

masculine singular:	**ce** bic
* if starting with vowel sound:	**cet** album
feminine singular:	**cette** bague
m & f plural:	**ces** bics

Stratégies!

★ getting tricky numbers right

★ using *monsieur* and *madame* when talking to adults

★ using time markers

★ looking words up in the glossary if necessary

★ extra! building up a description in a sequence of short steps

l'excursion, c'était **amusant** – *the trip was* **fun**
le film, c'était **amusant** – *the film was* **funny**

4 Les célébrités

4A Une discussion sur les stars

- say why you like different stars
- use the words for 'his'/'her'
- recognise words you've met before

Dans un e-mail de Kévin à Sadiq...

> Tu aimes quelles stars, Sadiq? Moi, j'aime l'acteur Melvil Poupaud.

quelles – *which*

> J'adore David Beckham.
> Il a beaucoup de talent.
> J'aime son look et ses vêtements.

> J'aime aussi Beyoncé.
> Elle a beaucoup de talent.
> J'aime sa musique et son look.

> Mes parents aiment Elvis Presley.
> Moi, je n'aime pas sa musique.
> Et je n'aime pas ses vêtements.

1 a 💿 **Écoute et lis.**

1 b ♻ **Stratégies!** *Recycling language from* **Voilà 2**

OK, so you've seen the words in red before: you remember words best by re-using them.

- With a partner:
  - Which red words can you remember?
  - *Son, sa* and *ses* all mean 'his' or 'her'.
  Look up any other words in the *Glossaire* (pp. 133–141).

1 c 💿 **Écoute les opinions (1–6). C'est qui?**

Exemple: **1 Beyoncé**

1 d 💬 **Lis les textes: A une phrase, B une phrase. Attention à la prononciation!**

j'aime	(aussi)	*name of star*
j'adore		son look
je n'aime pas		sa musique
		ses vêtements
il / elle a beaucoup de talent		

Grammaire: *son, sa, ses*

Remember the three words for 'my'?

These words follow the same pattern:
They mean both 'his' and 'her'.

the word that follows is...

	masculine	feminine	plural
	mon	*ma*	*mes*
	son	*sa*	*ses*

sa musique = his music **or** her music; *ses vêtements* = his clothes **or** her clothes

▼

2  **Does the red word mean 'his' or 'her'?**

Example: **1** *his*

1 J'adore Brad Pitt. J'aime ses films.

2 Elvis? Je n'aime pas son look.

3 J'aime Kylie, et j'aime sa sœur, Dani.

4 Graham Norton? J'aime ses talk-shows.

5 J'aime aussi J. K. Rowling: j'adore ses livres.

6 J'adore Marilyn Monroe! J'aime son look.

3 a **Discute de six stars avec ton/ta partenaire.**

Exemple:

A Tu aimes quelles stars?
B J'aime Tom Cruise. Il a beaucoup de talent. Et j'aime aussi...

3 b ✏ **Écris des phrases sur cinq stars.**

Exemple:

J'adore Avril Lavigne: j'aime sa musique.

4 📖 **Lis l'article. Note en anglais trois détails sur Melvil Poupaud.** ▶

Melvil Poupaud

● Melvil Poupaud est un acteur célèbre en France. Il a fait son premier film, *La ville des pirates*, à l'âge de dix ans!

● À 21 ans, il a écrit et réalisé un film.

réalisé – produced

● Et Melvil est aussi musicien: il a fait des albums avec son groupe, "Mud", et en solo. Eh oui, il a beaucoup de talent!

5 💿 **extra!** **Écoute les infos sur Vanessa Paradis, une star française. Choisis la bonne option.**

1 Vanessa habite à Paris avec...

   a Tom Cruise **b** Brad Pitt **c** Johnny Depp.

2 Son anniversaire, c'est...

   a le 22 novembre **b** le 22 décembre **c** le 22 janvier.

3 Vanessa a...

   a un frère **b** un frère et une sœur **c** une sœur.

4 Son premier film s'appelle...

   a *Noce blanche* **b** *Hollywood* **c** *Inferno*.

5 Pour son troisième album, Vanessa chante...

   a en français **b** en anglais **c** en italien.

4B Tes opinions

- give your opinion on various stars
- use adjectives
- connect sentences with *parce que* (because)

Moi, j'aime Jennifer Aniston, parce qu'elle est très belle et elle est amusante. J'aime ses vêtements et son look.

Ma star préférée, c'est P. Diddy. J'aime sa musique et ses vêtements. Il est très original et il est beau aussi.

Moi, j'adore le comique Sanjeev Bhaskar. Il est très amusant et original. Et il est intelligent aussi.

1 a 💿 Écoute et lis.

1 b 📖 C'est quoi en français? Regarde les mots en rouge!

Exemple: *good-looking (beautiful)* = belle

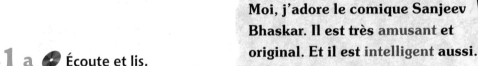

1 c 💿 Écoute les textes. Quand il y a une pause, répète le dernier mot.

Exemple: J'aime sa musique…   musique.

2 a ✏️ Identifie et écris les phrases!

1. Elle est intelligente, et belle aussi.   3. Il est très original et il est beau.

2. J'aime ses vêtements et son look.   4. Elle est amusante.

J'aime l'actrice australienne Nicole Kidman. Elle a beaucoup de talent. Elle est originale, intelligente, et belle aussi.

2 b ♻ **Grammaire: adjectives**

- How do you make most adjectives feminine?

  il est amusant → *elle est amusant* **?**

  il est original → *elle est original* **?**

- Remember these exceptions:

  beau = good-looking (male)

  belle = good-looking (female)

2 c 🖉 **Corrige l'erreur dans chaque phrase.**

Exemple: **1 Il est très amusant.**

1 Il est très ~~amusante~~.

2 Sa sœur, Anne, est ~~beau~~.

3 Mélanie est ~~original~~.

4 Et elle est assez ~~intelligent~~.

5 Son frère est ~~belle~~.

3 💿 **Écoute les discussions (1–5). Est-ce que *les deux* personnes aiment la star?**

Exemple: **1 oui**

4 🖉 **Écris une phrase avec *parce qu'il/parce qu'elle*.**

Exemple: **J'aime Ewan MacGregor parce qu'il est beau.**

1 J'aime Ewan MacGregor. Il est beau.

2 Et j'aime Zinédine Zidane. Il a beaucoup de talent.

3 J'adore Keira Knightley. Elle est belle.

4 Moi, j'aime beaucoup Mr Bean. Il est amusant.

5 J'aime Dawn French. Elle est originale.

5 💬 **A dit le nom d'une célébrité; B donne une opinion. Pas d'hésitation!**

Exemple: **A Eminem.**

        B Il est original.

6 🖉 **Écris ton opinion sur trois stars. Ton modèle: l'exercice 1.**

Stratégies! *parce que*

It can sound more natural to join two sentences into one with *parce que* (because):

J'aime P. Diddy. Il a beaucoup de talent.

*J'aime P. Diddy **parce qu'** il a beaucoup de talent.*

j'aime… parce qu'il / elle…		
il elle	est	amusant(e) / original(e) / intelligent(e) / beau (belle)
il elle	a	beaucoup de talent
j'aime je n'aime pas		son look / sa musique / ses vêtements

4C Styles de vie

- describe a person's lifestyle
- use negative sentences
- spot negatives in a listening activity

C'est **Health Week** ("la semaine de la santé") au collège de Sadiq à York. Pendant le cours de français, on analyse le style de vie des stars.

style de vie – *lifestyle*

A Ta star préférée, c'est qui?

B Il/Elle fume?

C Il/Elle fait beaucoup d'exercice?

D Il/Elle boit beaucoup d'alcool?

E Il/Elle mange beaucoup de fruits et de légumes?

F Il/Elle se drogue?

il se drogue – *he takes drugs*

1 a 💿 Écoute les six questions et note les lettres A–F dans le bon ordre.

Exemple: **A, E, ...**

1 b 📖 Trouve les paires: questions A–F et réponses 1–6.

Exemple: **A 6**

1 Non, du vin rouge, parfois. C'est tout.

2 Non, l'héroïne, etc., c'est trop dangereux.

3 Oui, il adore les carottes, les oranges, les bananes…

4 Oui, vingt cigarettes par jour. C'est idiot!

5 Oui, il fait du jogging, par exemple.

6 C'est Gino Ducastel.

2 ✏️ Trouve les paires.

Exemple: **A** Il mange beaucoup de fruits.

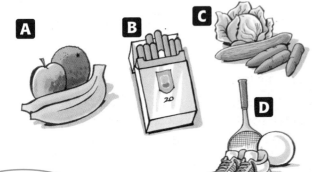

A **B** **C** **D** **E**

Il fait beaucoup d'exercice.
Elle boit beaucoup d'alcool.
Il fume.
Il mange beaucoup de fruits.
Elle mange beaucoup de légumes.

L'actrice **Pooja Shah** ne mange pas beaucoup de fast-food: elle préfère les fruits et les légumes. Elle boit beaucoup d'eau minérale.

Le célèbre footballeur, **Michael Owen**, ne boit pas, il ne fume pas, et il ne se drogue pas. Il fait beaucoup d'exercice. Il ne sort pas souvent le soir.

Homer Simpson adore le fast-food et il boit beaucoup de bière. Il ne fait pas d'exercice: le soir, il regarde la télé.

3 a 💿 Écoute et lis l'article.

3 b 🗨 Pose les questions **A–E** à ton/ta partenaire.
Réponds: *Oui / Non / Je ne sais pas*.

Exemple: **A** Elle fume, Pooja Shah?
B Je ne sais pas.

> **A** Il/Elle fume?
> **B** Il/Elle fait beaucoup d'exercice?
> **C** Il/Elle boit beaucoup d'alcool?
> **D** Il/Elle mange beaucoup de fruits et de légumes?
> **E** Il/Elle se drogue?

je ne sais pas – *I don't know*

4 a ♻ **Grammaire:** *le négatif*
Michael Owen ne boit pas.
- In your own words, write the rule for making sentences negative.
- Compare with your partner: have you written the same thing?

4 b 💿 Écoute (1–4). Écris *oui* ou *non*.
La personne... **a** mange des légumes?
b fait de l'exercice?
c boit de l'alcool?

Exemple: **1 a** oui; **b** non; **c** ...

◀ **Stratégies!** *Listening to the detail*
Don't miss the negative phrase if there is one: it makes all the difference!

elle mange...   she eats...
*elle **ne** mange **pas**...*   she **doesn't** eat...

5 🖊 **Décris le style de vie de deux personnes (ton père, une amie, etc.).**

Exemple: Mon amie Claire ne fume pas. Elle...

il	(ne) fume (pas) / (ne) se drogue (pas)	
elle	(ne) mange (pas)	beaucoup de fruits / légumes
	(ne) fait (pas)	beaucoup d'exercice
	(ne) boit (pas)	beaucoup d'alcool

4D Johnny Depp

- read a longer text about a star
- recognise more negative phrases

1 a Stratégies! *Class shared reading*

You can probably understand more than you think!

🔘 Read through and listen to the text together.

- Say in English the words you recognise.
- Look below the text for the meaning of words with an asterisk.

1 b 📖 On mentionne ces thèmes: oui ou non?

1 ses parents
2 ses animaux
3 son problème avec l'alcool
4 ses films
5 où il habite

1 c Grammaire: more negatives

ne (verb) *jamais* = never
ne (verb) *personne* = no one

    il **ne** fume **jamais** he never smokes
    il **n'**y a **personne** there is no one

- Find an example of each negative in the text and write the sentences in both French and English.

1 d 📖 Vrai ou faux?

1 *At school, Johnny took drugs.*
2 *He married Winona Ryder in 1993.*
3 *He spent a night in prison for vandalising a restaurant.*
4 *Johnny has lived in France since 1980.*
5 *He speaks French.*

1 e 📖 *Explain the pun in the last line!*

Johnny Depp: un Américain en France

L'acteur Johnny Depp est riche et célèbre. Mais il a eu* des problèmes dans la vie*…

Son père et sa mère se séparent* quand il est petit. À l'école, Johnny se drogue.

Johnny Depp et Winona Ryder sont un couple célèbre à Hollywood. Mais ils se séparent en 1993. C'est une période difficile pour Johnny. Il boit beaucoup d'alcool. Il n'y a personne* d'important dans sa vie.

Un soir, il vandalise sa chambre d'hôtel, et il passe la nuit* en prison.

Depuis* 1998, Johnny habite en France avec la star française, Vanessa Paradis. Il parle français.

Johnny a beaucoup changé. Il ne se drogue jamais. La vie avec Vanessa, c'est le paradis!

il a eu – *he has had*	personne – *nobody*
la vie – *life*	passe la nuit – *spends the night*
se séparent – *separate*	depuis – *since*

Johnny Depp et Vanessa Paradis

Une discussion sur les stars

j'aime…
j'aime aussi…
je n'aime pas…
j'adore…
  sa musique
  son look
  ses vêtements
il/elle a beaucoup de talent

A discussion about stars

I like…
I also like…
I don't like…
I love…
  his/her music
  his/her look/image
  his/her clothes
he/she is very talented

Tes opinions

j'aime…
parce qu'il/elle est…
  amusant(e)
  original(e)
  intelligent(e)
il est beau
elle est belle

Your opinions

I like…
because he/she is…
  funny
  original
  intelligent
he is good-looking/handsome
she is good-looking/beautiful

Styles de vie

il fume
il se drogue
il boit beaucoup d'alcool
elle mange…
  beaucoup de fruits
  beaucoup de légumes
elle fait beaucoup d'exercice
il ne fume pas
il ne se drogue pas
il ne boit pas beaucoup
  d'alcool
elle ne mange pas beaucoup
  de fruits
elle ne fait pas beaucoup
  d'exercice

Lifestyles

he smokes
he takes drugs
he drinks a lot of alcohol
she eats…
  a lot of fruit
  a lot of vegetables
she does a lot of exercise
he doesn't smoke
he doesn't take drugs
*he doesn't drink a lot of
  alcohol*
*she doesn't eat a lot of
  fruit*
*she doesn't do a lot of
  exercise*

Grammaire:

- his/her
  These three words can all
  mean *either* 'his' or 'her':
  son + masc. singular noun
  sa + fem. singular noun
  ses + plural noun

- adjectives
  – add an **e** for feminine
  – exceptions: *beau* (m)/*belle* (f)

- negatives
  – put **ne** ... **pas** round the verb
  – other negative forms:
  ne (verb) **jamais** never
  ne (verb) **personne** no one

Stratégies!

★ recycling language from *Voilà 2*

★ connecting sentences with *parce que* (because)

★ listening to the detail: spotting negative phrases

★ understanding a longer text by looking for words you recognise and using translations given with the text

une **personne** – *one person*
un ... **personne** – *no-one*

Stratégies! *Preparing for your assessment*

- Your revision will be more efficient (and faster!) if you focus only on what you *don't* know. Go through the *Sommaire* worksheets for units 3 and 4 (sheets 25 and 37), and highlight in yellow the words you *can't* remember.

- Learn three of these words each night. When you know them, highlight them in red.

1 a 📖 **Au magasin de souvenirs. Écris les lettres dans le bon ordre.**

Exemple: **E, C, ...**

1 b ✏️ **Écris le dialogue, et change les mots en rouge.**

1 c 💬 **Joue ton dialogue avec ton/ta partenaire.**

2 💿 **Écoute la conversation. Note les lettres A–E dans le bon ordre.**

A – C'est tout, monsieur?

B – Alors, six euros cinquante, monsieur.

C – C'est six euros cinquante.

D – Voilà. Merci, madame. Au revoir.

E – Pardon, madame. C'est combien, cette bague?

F – C'est bon.

G – Oui, c'est tout.

 A
 B
 **C**
 **D**
 **E**

3 📖 **Lis l'article. C'est vrai (V) ou faux (F)?**

Exemple: **1 F**

1 Philippe est prof de maths.
2 Il est intelligent.
3 Philippe fait beaucoup d'exercice.
4 Il boit beaucoup d'alcool.
5 Il adore le fast-food.
6 Philippe aime les vêtements de Marc.

Philippe Longy

Philippe est acteur dans une série. Il est beau, intelligent et il a beaucoup de talent.

"Mon look est très important," dit Philippe. "Le soir, je fais beaucoup d'exercice. J'adore le sport: je joue au football. Je ne bois pas d'alcool: je préfère le jus de fruits. Et je n'aime pas le fast-food."

Philippe joue le rôle de Marc Duhamel. "J'aime mon rôle. Marc est amusant, mais je n'aime pas ses vêtements!"

Les Impressionnistes

L'art traditionnel...

Voici une peinture traditionnelle de 1847.

Le thème est historique. Les personnages sont des héros mythiques.

Les couleurs? Des couleurs calmes et sombres (bruns, noirs, etc.).

> une peinture – *a painting*
> les personnages – *the people in it*
> héros mythiques – *mythical heroes*

Les Romains de la Décadence,
Thomas Couture (1847)

... et l'art impressionniste

L'impressionnisme, c'est une révolte contre la tradition.

Regarde l'exemple ci-dessous. Le thème (un café) est moderne pour 1881.

Les personnages sont des gens ordinaires.

Les couleurs sont dynamiques (rouges, jaunes, bleus, verts...).

> contre – *against*
> gens – *people*

Le Déjeuner des Canotiers,
Pierre-Auguste Renoir (1880–1881)

Un artiste impressionniste très célèbre, c'est Vincent van Gogh (1853–1890).

Il était hollandais, mais il a habité en France, à Paris, et puis dans le sud de la France.

Van Gogh était pauvre, mais en 1987, un collectionneur a acheté sa peinture *Les Tournesols (Sunflowers)* pour 49 millions de dollars!

> pauvre – *poor*

Vase avec douze tournesols,
Vincent van Gogh (1888)

1 *Identify the styles: traditional or impressionist?*

1 *historical themes*
2 *modern themes*
3 *calm colours*
4 *ordinary people*
5 *lively, dynamic colours*

2 **Tu préfères quelle peinture sur cette page?**

> Je préfère la peinture numéro...

5 La France et le tourisme

5A Les magasins

- learn the names of shops
- ask if there's a shop nearby
- use the glossary

Imagine: tu es touriste à Biarritz. Tu es en ville.

> Pardon, madame. Il y a une pâtisserie près d'ici?
> *Is there a cake shop near here?*

B une pâtisserie

C une boucherie

A une boulangerie

E une pharmacie

D une charcuterie

F un tabac

G un supermarché

1 a 💿 Écoute et note les lettres dans le bon ordre.

Exemple: **B, …**

1 b ✏ Écris les magasins en français et en anglais.

Exemple: **un tabac – a *tobacconist's/newsagent***

un tab- une bouch- une pharm-	-isserie -erie
un super- **une boulan-**	-acie **-ac** -gerie
une char- une pât-	-marché **-cuterie**

2 a 💿 Écoute et lis le dialogue. C'est quoi, la prononciation de "dix"?

> ▶ **A** Pardon, monsieur. Il y a une boucherie près d'ici?
> **B** Oui, dans la rue Jeanne d'Arc.
> **A** C'est loin?
> **B** Non, c'est à **dix** minutes.
> **A** Merci, monsieur. Au revoir.

2 b 💿 **Écoute (1–3).**

Le magasin est à combien de minutes? extra! Note aussi le magasin + la rue.

Exemple: **1 à 2 minutes** (extra! une charcuterie, rue Victoria)

3 a ✏️ **Écris deux des dialogues A–D.** ▶

Exemple:

- Pardon, madame. Il y a un/une ___ près d'ici?
- Oui, dans la rue ___.
- C'est loin?
- Non, c'est à ___ minutes.
- Merci, madame. Au revoir.

3 b 💬 **Joue les quatre dialogues.**

4 ♻️✏️ extra! **Note d'autres destinations.**

> 6 destinations = bien!
> 10 destinations = super!

Fais un chemin de mots:

```
        p
        a
centre  commercial
        c
```

5 📖 **Lis le texte et note les parfums de dix glaces en français et en anglais.**

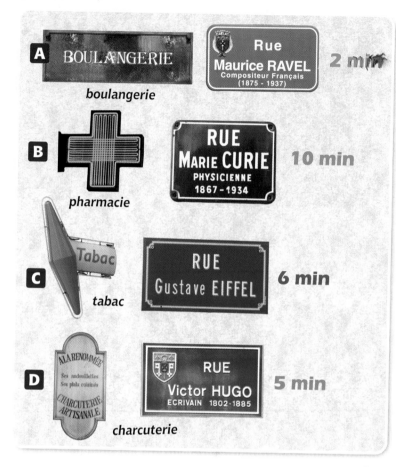

A BOULANGERIE — boulangerie — Rue Maurice RAVEL Compositeur Français (1875 - 1937) — 2 min

B pharmacie — RUE MARIE CURIE PHYSICIENNE 1867-1934 — 10 min

C Tabac — tabac — RUE Gustave EIFFEL — 6 min

D ALA RENOMMÉE Ses andouillettes Ses plats cuisinés CHARCUTERIE ARTISANALE — charcuterie — RUE Victor HUGO ECRIVAIN 1802-1885 — 5 min

L'année dernière, je suis allé chez mon cousin à Nice. Nice, c'est bien: j'aime la plage et j'aime les restaurants et les magasins.

Un jour, mon cousin et moi, on a acheté une glace à DIX boules: citron, banane, cassis, pomme, menthe, orange, café, chocolat blanc, noisette et fraise! Miam-miam! C'était bon!

Kévin

pardon monsieur / madame	
il y a une boulangerie près d'ici?	
une boucherie / une pâtisserie / une charcuterie une pharmacie / un tabac / un supermarché	
oui, dans la rue *Jeanne d'Arc*	
c'est loin?	c'est à dix minutes
merci, monsieur	au revoir

Stratégies! *Le Glossaire*

If you're stuck, remember to look up new words in the glossary.

5B Un touriste à Biarritz

- ask what you can do in a holiday resort
- ask for a brochure at the tourist office
- use *on peut* with the infinitive

A *À Biarritz, on peut faire du surf*

B *On peut faire du cheval*

C *On peut louer des vélos*

1 a **Écoute: c'est quelle photo (A–F)?**

1 b 💬 **A dit une phrase; B identifie la photo.**

Exemple: **A On peut aller à la plage.**
            B C'est la photo E.

 on peut… – you can…

2 ✏️ **Écris six phrases avec le bon verbe.**

Exemple: **1 À Biarritz, on peut *faire* du surf.**

À Biarritz, on peut	**?**	du surf
		à la plage
		du karting
		du cheval
		des vélos
		des excursions

à Biarritz…

on peut	faire	du cheval
		du surf
		du karting
		des excursions
	aller	à la plage
	louer	des vélos

Grammaire: *on peut* you can

- After **on peut** use the *infinitive* (the form of the verb you find in the dictionary):
  *on peut **louer** des vélos* you can hire bikes
- Note: these infinitives end in **-er** or **-re**.

3 ✏️ **Écris une brochure sur Biarritz. Tu trouves des photos sur Internet?**

ou extra! ♻️ **Écris une brochure sur *ta* ville.**

Exemple:

Remember to use the infinitive with all verbs, e.g. *je joue* ➞ *on peut jou**er***

À Wolverhampton…
…on peut aller au cinéma.
…on peut faire du judo.
…on peut jouer au basket.

D *On peut faire du karting*

E *On peut aller à la plage*

F *On peut faire des excursions*

4 a 💿 **Écoute et lis.** ▶

Madame Cassou, la mère de Kévin et d'Estelle, travaille à l'office du tourisme.

Mme Cassou	Bonjour, monsieur. Je peux vous aider?
Touriste	Oui. On peut faire du karting à Biarritz?
Mme Cassou	Oui, bien sûr.
Touriste	Avez-vous une brochure?
Mme Cassou	Oui, monsieur. Voilà.

4 b ✏️ **Écris les phrases en français.**

1 *Can I help you?*
2 *Yes, of course.*
3 *Do you have a brochure?*
4 *Here you are.*

4 c 💬 **Joue le dialogue. Change la phrase en rouge.**

> je peux vous aider?
> on peut *faire du karting* à Biarritz?
> oui, bien sûr
> avez-vous une brochure?
> oui, monsieur. voilà

5 📖 **Lis le texte et réponds en anglais.**

1 *Where does the train leave from?*
2 *Does it go to the town centre?*
3 *Can you use it in April? In July? In October?*
4 *How frequently does it leave?*
5 *When does the first train leave?*

Le Petit Train de Biarritz

De la Grande Plage à la Côte des Basques, en passant par le Port des Pêcheurs et le centre-ville, le Petit Train offre une visite commentée de Biarritz, sans fatigue, et sans problèmes de parking.

De début avril à fin octobre, départ Grande Plage: toutes les 30 minutes, tous les jours à partir de 14h.

5C La France touristique

- find out more about France

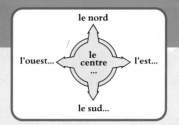

Moi, c'est Caroline.

J'habite à Metz, dans l'est de la France. C'est une grande ville industrielle. Il y a beaucoup de grandes villes dans la région. Il n'y a pas beaucoup de touristes!

À Metz, on peut aller au cinéma. On peut faire des excursions en Allemagne et au Luxembourg. Mais on ne peut pas faire de surf!

En été, il y a beaucoup de touristes

Salut. Je m'appelle Julien.

J'habite à La Rochelle, dans l'ouest de la France. C'est une belle ville historique. En été, il fait beau et il y a beaucoup de touristes. Ils aiment les belles plages.

À La Rochelle, on peut faire du surf. On peut aussi faire des excursions. La Rochelle, c'est super!

Salut. Moi, je m'appelle Émilie.

J'habite à Besse, dans le Massif Central. C'est dans le centre de la France. Dans le Massif Central, il y a beaucoup de collines vertes. On peut faire du cheval et on peut louer des vélos. Il y a beaucoup de petits villages et il n'y a pas beaucoup de touristes. C'est génial!

Il n'y a pas beaucoup de touristes

salut	je m'appelle…	
j'habite à *La Rochelle*		
dans l'ouest / l'est / le sud / le nord / le centre		de la France
il y a / il n'y a pas	beaucoup de touristes	
on peut… / on peut aussi…		

1 a 🔘 **Écoute et lis les textes de la page 46, un par un. Réponds aux questions.**

Julien: **1** *What's the weather like in La Rochelle in summer?*

           2 *Which two activities does Julien mention?*

Caroline: **1** *What sort of a town is Metz?*

           2 *Which countries can you get to easily from Metz?*

Émilie: **1** *Which of the following can you find in the Massif Central?*

              a *green hills*   **b** *beautiful beaches*   **c** *little villages*   **d** *big industrial towns*

           2 *Which two activities does Émilie mention?*

1 b 📖 **Regarde la photo. C'est La Rochelle ou Metz?**

2 a 🔘 **Écoute et lis le dialogue avec Julien.**

> **1** – Comment t'appelles-tu?
>   – Je m'appelle Julien.
>
> **2** – Où habites-tu?
>   – J'habite à La Rochelle, dans l'ouest de la France.
>
> **3** – Il y a beaucoup de touristes?
>   – Oui, il y a beaucoup de touristes.
>
> **4** – On peut faire des excursions?
>   – Oui, bien sûr. Et on peut aussi faire du surf.

2 b 💬 **Joue le dialogue. Puis joue deux dialogues similaires pour Caroline et Émilie.**

2 c 🔘 extra! **Écoute une autre personne. Note les réponses aux quatre questions.**

Exemple: **1** Anne. 2 …

● 📖 **Puis, regarde tes réponses et écris le dialogue avec Anne.**

3 a 📖 **Quiz sur la France 🇫🇷 et le Royaume-Uni 🇬🇧**

C'est la France ou le Royaume-Uni?

1 a 550 000 km²
   b 244 000 km²

2 a 59 millions d'habitants
   b 60 millions d'habitants

> 1 000 000 = **un million**
> 1 000 = **mille**
> 100 = **cent**
> 40 500 000
>   = quarante millions, cinq cent mille
> 2000 km²
>   = deux mille kilomètres **carrés**

3 b 🔘 **Écoute et vérifie tes réponses.**

5D Une carte postale

- revise weather expressions
- read and write holiday postcards
- use *très* and *vraiment* for emphasis

Biarritz

1 ♻ 📖 Quel temps fait-il? Trouve les paires.

Exemple: **A** il fait froid

| il pleut | il fait chaud | il fait froid |
| il neige | il fait beau | il fait mauvais |

A **B** **C** **D** **E** **F**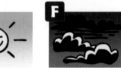

2 💬 A pose une question (1–4); B répond avec *vraiment* ou *très*.

Il fait... 1 chaud? 2 beau? 3 froid? 4 mauvais?

Exemple: **A** Il fait chaud?
B Oui, il fait vraiment chaud!

Stratégies! *Adding emphasis*

Use *vraiment* and *très* to give emphasis:
*il fait **très** chaud*   it's **very** hot
*il fait **vraiment** froid*   it's **really** cold

3 a 💿 Écoute et lis les cartes postales.
Puis regarde les images 1–6. C'est Nina ou Louis?

1 **2** **3**

5  **4**  **6**

3 b 💿 Écoute les deux cartes postales de Nina et Louis. Il y a une différence? Lève la main.

4 a ✏️ Deux touristes en Grande-Bretagne...

Invente et écris deux cartes postales: une 🙂 et une 🙁 . Tes modèles: Nina et Louis.

4 b ✏️ Ton/Ta partenaire vérifie tes cartes postales. Puis corrige tes erreurs.

> Salut! Ça va?
> Je suis à Biarritz. C'est vraiment fantastique ici. On peut aller à la plage et on peut aussi faire du surf. Il fait très chaud.
> À bientôt!
> Nina

> Salut!
> Je suis à Orcières, dans les Alpes. C'est vraiment nul ici! On peut faire du ski? Non! Il pleut et il fait très froid, mais il ne neige pas!
> À bientôt!
> Louis

il pleut / il neige			
il fait	très vraiment	chaud / froid beau / mauvais	
je suis à...			
c'est	vraiment	fantastique nul	ici
à bientôt			

Les magasins	The shops
pardon, monsieur	*excuse me* (to a man)
pardon, madame	*excuse me* (to a woman)
il y a une boulangerie près d'ici?	*is there a baker's shop near here?*
une boucherie	*a butcher's shop*
une pâtisserie	*a cake shop*
une charcuterie	*a delicatessen*
une pharmacie	*a chemist's*
un tabac	*a tobacconist's/newsagent*
un supermarché	*a supermarket*
oui, dans la rue...	*yes, in... Street*
c'est loin?	*is it far?*
c'est à dix minutes	*it's 10 minutes away*
merci	*thank you*
au revoir	*goodbye*

Un touriste à Biarritz	A tourist in Biarritz
à Biarritz	*in Biarritz*
on peut...	*you can...*
faire du cheval	*go horse-riding*
faire du surf	*go surfing*
faire du karting	*go go-karting*
faire des excursions	*go on trips*
aller à la plage	*go to the beach*
louer des vélos	*hire bikes*
je peux vous aider?	*can I help you?*
on peut faire du karting à Biarritz?	*can you go go-karting in Biarritz?*
oui, bien sûr	*yes, of course*
avez-vous une brochure?	*do you have a brochure?*
voilà	*here you are*

La France touristique	Tourist France
salut	*hi*
je m'appelle	*my name is*
j'habite à...	*I live in...*
dans...	*in...*
l'ouest	*the west*
l'est	*the east*
le sud	*the south*
le nord	*the north*
le centre	*the centre*
de la France	*of France*
il y a beaucoup de touristes	*there are lots of tourists*
il n'y a pas beaucoup de touristes	*there aren't a lot of tourists*
on peut...	*you can...*
on peut aussi...	*you can also...*

Une carte postale	A postcard
il pleut	*it's raining*
il neige	*it's snowing*
il fait très chaud	*it's very hot*
il fait froid	*it's cold*
il fait beau	*it's nice weather*
il fait mauvais	*it's bad weather*
je suis à...	*I'm in...*
c'est vraiment nul ici	*it's really awful here*
fantastique	*fantastic*
à bientôt	*see you soon*

Grammaire:

- **on peut** (you can) is used with the *infinitive* (the form of the verb you find in the dictionary):
  on peut **louer** des vélos you can hire bikes

1 word
2 meanings
à Biarritz – **in** *Biarritz*
à dix minutes – *ten minutes* **away**

Stratégies!

★ looking up words in the glossary if you're stuck

★ using *vraiment* (really) and *très* (very) to add emphasis to a sentence

6 Problèmes

6A Aïe! J'ai mal...

- say what's wrong with you
- use *au*, *à la*, etc. correctly

Cette peinture célèbre, "La Joconde", est au musée du Louvre à Paris. Elle s'appelle comment en anglais?

Le peintre italien, Léonard de Vinci, a habité en France de 1516 à 1519.

Mais la "star" a des problèmes...

A à la tête

C à la main

D à l'estomac

G au genou

H aux pieds

Aïe! J'ai mal...

à la gorge **B**

au bras **E**

au dos **F**

1 💿 Écoute et lis. Note les lettres (A–H) dans le bon ordre.

2 a ♻ Grammaire: *au, à la, à l', aux*

j'ai mal à la gorge = (I have an ache 'at' the throat) = I have a sore throat

- Match each word on the left with a category on the right.

au	*à la*	followed by	a feminine word	a singular word beginning with a vowel
à l'	*aux*		a plural word	a masculine word

- Check your answers on page 130.

2 b ✏ Écris six phrases.

Exemple: **1** J'ai mal à la main.

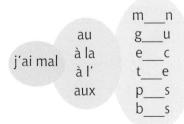

j'ai mal

au
à la
à l'
aux

m___n
g___u
e___c
t___e
p___s
b___s

Où avez-vous mal?

3 a 💿 Écoute (1–8). C'est quelle image (A–H)?

Exemple: **1 E**

3 b 💬 Joue un petit dialogue pour chaque image (A–H).

Exemple: **A**
A Salut! Ça va?
B Non. J'ai mal *à la gorge*.
A Oh là là!

3 c ✏️ Écris une phrase pour chaque image.

Exemple: **1 J'ai mal à la gorge.**

ça va?	non, j'ai mal	au	bras / dos / genou
		à la	tête / gorge / main
		à l'	estomac
		aux	pieds

4 📖 extra! Détective de langue! Lis l'article.

1 *Find the French for:*

   a *body (**Tip:** think of the English word for a dead body)*

   b *nerve cells (**Tip:** word order is often reversed in French)*

2 *What quantity of the following is found in the body of an adult?*

   a *water*   **d** *nerve cells*

   b *air*   **e** *food in the stomach*

   c *muscles*

▶

Quelques chiffres

Voici ce qu'on peut trouver dans le corps d'un adulte:

● **4 à 5 litres de sang,**

● **45 litres d'eau,**

● **2,5 litres d'air dans les poumons,**

● **0,5 litre de nourriture dans l'estomac,**

● **206 os pour un total d'environ 10 kilos,**

● **650 muscles environ,**

● **13 milliards de cellules nerveuses.**

un milliard = mille millions
le sang – *blood*

- understand a play
- act out a radio play

Les problèmes de M. Blanc
une pièce de théâtre

Personnages:

- narrateur
- M. Blanc
- son patron (his boss)

A M. Blanc habite à Paris. Il adore le tennis.

Lundi dernier, il a téléphoné à son bureau.

M. Blanc: Je ne peux pas venir travailler. J'ai mal à la tête.

Le patron: Pas de problème, M. Blanc.

venir travailler –
to come to work

B Mardi, M. Blanc a téléphoné à son bureau.

M. Blanc: Je ne peux pas venir travailler. J'ai mal à l'estomac. J'ai vomi.

Le patron: Pas de problème.

Mais M. Blanc est allé au stade. C'était le célèbre tournoi de tennis de Roland-Garros!

C Mercredi matin...

M. Blanc: Je ne peux pas venir travailler. J'ai mal au dos.

Le patron: Hmm!

Jeudi matin...

M. Blanc: J'ai mal à la gorge.

Le patron: Oh là là!

Vendredi matin...

M. Blanc: J'ai mal aux pieds.

Le patron: Mais c'est ridicule!!

Mal à la gorge? Mal aux pieds? Non! M. Blanc est allé regarder le tennis!

D Lundi, M. Blanc est allé au bureau.

Le patron: Ah! M. Blanc! Ça va?

M. Blanc: Oui, ça va bien, merci. Mais la semaine dernière, c'était horrible! Je...

Le patron: M. Blanc! Regardez cette photo!

M. Blanc: Mais...

Le patron: Vous êtes allé regarder le tennis! Vous êtes renvoyé!

renvoyé – *sacked*

1 a 💿 *Class shared listening and reading. Read and listen to the play on page 52.*

Section A: **1**   *What did M. Blanc do on Monday last week?*

          2   *What was his excuse for not going to work?*

Section B: **3**   *What was his excuse on Tuesday?*

          4   *Where did he go?*

Section C: **5**   *What were his excuses on Wednesday, Thursday and Friday?*

Section D: **6**   *How did the boss know M. Blanc hadn't been ill?*

          7   *What happened to M. Blanc at the end?*

1 b 💿 **Recopie les jours:**

**Écoute une version différente.
Note l'excuse pour chaque jour.**

Exemple: **lundi – mal à la main**

> lundi
> mardi
> mercredi
> jeudi
> vendredi

2 ✏️ **Trouve les paires et écris les phrases, en français et en anglais.**

Exemple: **1 M. Blanc a téléphoné à son bureau. – *M. Blanc phoned his office.***

1   M. Blanc a téléphoné   à la gorge.

2   Mais M. Blanc est allé   le tennis!

3   J'ai mal   au stade.

4   Mais la semaine dernière,   c'était horrible!

5   Vous êtes allé regarder   à son bureau.

3 Stratégies! *Acting out a radio play*

- Work in threes, and take a role each.

- Practise *your* lines.
  - Ask for help with any words you're not sure how to pronounce.
  - Try to make your lines sound lively and interesting.

- Practise the play as a group.

- When you're ready, record your play.

extra! Change any details you like, for example change the excuses.

4 💬 **Discussion en classe.**

- *What French sporting events do you know?*
- *What do you know about them?*

Examples: **1 French Open (Roland-Garros)
tennis tournament, in May–June
2 Tour de France, ...**

- say how long you've been unwell
- ask if you can (still) go out

1 a **Écoute et lis le dialogue. C'est quoi en français?**

1 *are you OK?*	**4** *for four or five days*
2 *my back hurts*	**5** *for a week*
3 *for a long time?*	**6** *that's no joke*

Mme Cassou	Salut, Estelle. Ça va?
Estelle	Non! J'ai mal au dos.
Mme Cassou	Mal au dos? Depuis longtemps?
Estelle	Depuis quatre ou cinq jours... Non, depuis une semaine.
Mme Cassou	Hmm... Ce n'est pas amusant, ça!

1 b Joue et adapte le dialogue. **Change les mots en rouge et en bleu.**

au bras	au dos	deux jours
au genou	à la tête	trois jours
à la gorge	à la main	une semaines
à l'estomac	aux pieds	deux semaine

depuis longtemps? – (have you had it) for a long time?

1 c Écris un dialogue.

2 Écoute (1–4) et note la "route" du dialogue (quatre lettres).

Exemple: **1 C, F, ..., ...**

Bonjour, Antoine. Ça va?

Non. J'ai mal **A** à la gorge. **B** au bras. **C** à l'estomac. **D** aux pieds. **E** au dos.

Ah oui? Depuis longtemps?

Depuis **F** trois jours. **G** une semaine. **H** deux semaines.

Hmm... Ce n'est pas amusant, ça.

Maman, je peux **I** aller à la soirée ce soir? **J** jouer dans le match de foot samedi?

K Oui, bien sûr.   **L** Hmm... Je ne sais pas.

je ne sais pas – I don't know

3 ✏️ Identifie et recopie les phrases. Puis écris la phrase en anglais.

Exemple: **1** J'ai mal aux pieds. – *My feet hurt.*

1 J'ai mal aux pieds.   **3** Depuis deux jours.   **5** Je peux aller à la soirée samedi?

2 Depuis longtemps?   **4** Ce n'est pas amusant, ça.   **6** Hmm... Je ne sais pas.

4 a 💬 Regarde l'exercice 2. Joue quatre dialogues différents.

4 b ✏️ Écris deux dialogues.

5 💿 Quatre personnes ont un problème. Écoute et note en anglais:

    a le problème   **b** extra! la cause.

j'ai mal	au bras / à la gorge
	à l'estomac / aux pieds
depuis	longtemps?
	un jour / une semaine
ce n'est pas amusant, ça	
je peux	aller à la soirée ce soir?
	jouer dans le match de foot samedi?
oui, bien sûr	je ne sais pas

Sommaire

Aïe! J'ai mal...	Ouch! My... hurts	Ça va? Non!	Are you OK? No!
ça va?	*are you all right?*	depuis longtemps?	*(have you had it) for a long time?*
j'ai mal au bras	*my arm aches / hurts*		
j'ai mal au dos	*my back aches*	depuis...	*for...*
j'ai mal au genou	*my knee hurts*	un jour	*one day*
j'ai mal à la tête	*I have a headache*	une semaine	*one week*
j'ai mal à la gorge	*I have a sore throat*	ce n'est pas amusant, ça	*that's no joke*
j'ai mal à la main	*my hand hurts*	je peux...	*can I...*
j'ai mal à l'estomac	*I have stomach ache*	aller à la soirée?	*go to the party?*
j'ai mal aux pieds	*I've got sore feet*	jouer dans le match de foot?	*play in the football match?*
		ce soir	*this evening*
		samedi	*on Saturday*
		oui, bien sûr	*yes, of course*
		je ne sais pas	*I don't know*

Grammaire: *au, à la, à l', aux*

● talking about aches and pains:

    j'ai mal...   ***au*** + masculine noun   ***à la*** + feminine noun
            (***à l'*** if the noun begins with a vowel)
            aux + masc. or fem. plural noun

1 word
2 meanings
ça va **bien** – *I am well*
oui, **bien sûr** – *yes, of course*

Stratégies!

★ acting out a play: making your part sound lively and interesting

Stratégies! *Preparing for your assessment*

- Look back at the *Sommaire* pages for unit 5 (p. 49) and unit 6 (p. 55) and select up to ten words you can't remember very well.

- Make a small 'memory card' for each one: write the French on one side and the English on the other. Use the cards to practise: read one side and say the word on the other side from memory.

1 a 📖 **Lis la carte postale. Réponds en anglais.** ▶

1 *Where is La Rochelle?*
2 *What is the weather like?*
3 *How far away is the beach?*
4 *What two other activities does Andréa mention?*
5 *What kind of shop is there near the hotel?*

> Salut!
>
> Je suis à La Rochelle, dans l'ouest de la France. C'est vraiment fantastique ici, et il fait très chaud. La plage est à dix minutes à pied! On peut aussi faire du cheval et faire des excursions. Il y a beaucoup de touristes.
>
> Il y a une pâtisserie super près de l'hôtel, et je mange un éclair au chocolat tous les jours!
>
> À bientôt!
>
> Andréa

1 b ✏️ **Invente une carte postale. Écris 3–4 phrases.**

Exemple:

> Salut! Je suis à Strasbourg, dans l'est de la France. C'est vraiment génial ici. Il fait très froid. On peut faire du karting.
> À bientôt! Léa

2 a 💿 **Écoute (1–5). C'est quelle image (A–H)?**

Exemple: **1 H**

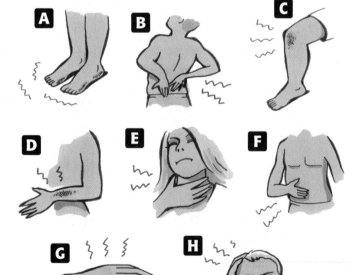

2 b 💿 **Depuis longtemps? Réécoute, et note les réponses.**

Exemple: **1 5 jours**   … jour(s) / … semaine(s)

3 💬 **Lis le dialogue. Puis joue trois dialogues similaires.**

– Bonjour, Thomas. Ça va?
– Non. J'ai mal au genou.
– Depuis longtemps?
– Depuis deux semaines.

3 jours

4 jours

1 semaine

Mathieu Villeroy adore la voile

Accident en mer

Mathieu Villeroy, 28 ans, adore la voile. Le vendredi 16 février 2004, il a quitté le port de Concarneau à 13h. L'océan était assez calme.

Mais soudain, à 16h, son mât a craqué, son bateau s'est retourné, et Mathieu Villeroy était dans l'eau!

> le mât – *mast*
> craquer – *to crack*
> le bateau – *boat*
> se retourner – *to overturn*

1 True or false?

a Mathieu set sail on Friday 16th February.

b The sea was very rough.

c The accident happened at 4pm.

d He spent six hours in the water.

e He managed to phone the police.

f He was found and taken to hospital.

2 Write a phrase from the text for each picture (A–D).

Example: **A – le mât a craqué**

Mathieu n'a pas paniqué.
Il s'est attaché à son bateau, et il a passé six heures dans l'eau froide.

Ses amis ont alerté la police à 18h30.

Finalement, un hélicoptère de la Marine nationale a retrouvé Mathieu, dans la mer, près de la côte, à 22h.

L'hélicoptère a transporté Mathieu à l'hôpital. Il a quitté l'hôpital samedi après-midi.

> s'est attaché à – *tied himself to*

7 Sadiq en France

7A Le dîner chez les Cassou

- understand offers of food and drink
- say you're hungry or thirsty

la viande

l'eau

le jus d'orange

Sadiq, tu aimes les gâteaux au chocolat?

les pommes de terre

les gâteaux au chocolat

la soupe

les pâtes

Oh, oui. J'aime ça.

1 a 💿 **Écoute (1–8). Note les lettres A–H dans le bon ordre.**

Exemple: **1 B**

1 b 💬 **A dit le mot en français; B dit le mot en anglais**
(sans regarder?! *without looking?!*).

Exemple: **A** la soupe
    B soup

les carottes

2 ✏️ **C'est quoi? Écris les mots 1–8.**

Exemple: **1 la viande**

3 ♻️ ✏️ extra! *How many other foods and drinks can you remember?*

Exemple: **le pain, le lait, …**

    4 mots: bien
    8 mots: très bien
    12 mots: super!

4  **Lis le texte. Réponds en anglais.**

1 *Who has Sadiq travelled with?*

2 *How did they travel to Biarritz?*

3 *How long is Sadiq going to stay?*

Sadiq est à Biarritz avec un groupe d'élèves de York, et trois profs de son collège.

Le groupe a quitté York le matin à sept heures. À Londres, ils ont pris le train pour Paris. Ils ont changé de train à Paris, et ils sont arrivés à Biarritz le soir, vers 20 heures.

Sadiq va passer une semaine chez Kévin. Ce soir, il dîne avec la famille Cassou.

5 a 💿 **Sadiq est à table avec la famille. Écoute et lis le dialogue.**

Before eating, French people wish each other "*bon appétit!*" (enjoy your meal).

toute la famille:	Bon appétit!
Mme Cassou:	Tu as faim, Sadiq?
Sadiq:	Oui, j'ai faim.
Estelle:	Tu aimes les carottes?
Sadiq:	Oh oui, beaucoup.
M. Cassou:	Tu as soif, Sadiq?
Sadiq:	Oui, j'ai soif.
M. Cassou:	Tu aimes le jus d'orange?
Sadiq:	Non, pas beaucoup. Je préfère l'eau.

5 b 📖 **C'est quoi en français?**

1 *enjoy your meal*   **4** *are you thirsty?*

2 *are you hungry?*   **5** *no, not much*

3 *do you like... ?*   **6** *I prefer...*

5 c Grammaire: expressions with *avoir*

J'ai means 'I have', but in these phrases, it means 'I am':

I am 14 = ***j'ai** 14 ans*

I am hungry = *j'ai* ❓

I am thirsty = ❓ *soif*

bon appétit	
tu as faim / soif?	oui, j'ai faim / soif
j'aime tu aimes… ?	les gâteaux au chocolat / le jus d'orange la soupe / la viande / l'eau / les pâtes les carottes / les pommes de terre
oui, beaucoup	non, pas beaucoup
je préfère *le jus d'orange*	

5 d 💬 **Joue et adapte le dialogue (ex. 5a).**

5 e ✏️ **Écris un dialogue similaire.**

6 💿 **Écoute les dialogues (1–5). Recopie et complète la grille.**

	faim?	soif?
1	oui	non
2		

7B Conversations à table

- ask if someone can pass you something
- chat at the table
- use the right word for 'please'

> Je peux avoir le pain, s'il vous plaît, Madame Cassou?

> Oui, voilà, Sadiq.

> Je peux avoir le fromage, s'il te plaît, Estelle?

> Oui, voilà.

je peux avoir... ? – can I have... ?

1 ♻ Stratégies!

Saying 'please' to different people

Read the two dialogues.
S'il te plaît and *s'il vous plaît* both mean 'please'.

- Which do you use when speaking to young people? And which when speaking to adults?

2 a ✏ Trouve les paires: la lettre A–H et le mot.

Exemple: **D** le lait

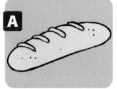   

les biscuits   le lait   le beurre

les frites   le pain   le thé

le fromage   le jambon

2 b 💿 Écoute huit questions à table. Note les lettres A–H.

Exemple: **1 A**

3 a 💬 Joue les mini-dialogues 1–4.

A Je peux avoir..., s'il te plaît/s'il vous plaît?

B Oui, voilà.

3 b ✏ Écris deux dialogues.

Exemple: – **Je peux avoir... ?**
            – **Oui, ...**

4 a Stratégies! *Real conversations*

At the table, the conversation can cover a range of topics. Be prepared!

🎧 **Écoute et lis la conversation. Sections A, B, C, D du diagramme, c'est quel thème?**

Exemple: **A la famille**

Thèmes: le collège   la télé
la ville   les sports   la famille

– Bon appétit!
– Tu as faim, Sadiq? Tu aimes la viande?
– Oh oui, beaucoup.

A
– Tu as des frères et sœurs, Sadiq?
– Oui, j'ai un frère et une sœur.

B
– Le prof de maths est sympa?
– Bof... ça va. Mais, j'aime les maths.

– Tu as soif, Estelle?
– Non, merci.

C
– Tu aimes les émissions de sport?
– Oui, et j'aime aussi les comédies.

D
– Tu fais du vélo, Sadiq?
– Oui. Et je joue aussi au cricket.

– Je peux avoir les pommes de terre, s'il vous plaît?
– Voilà.
– Merci.

4 b 🎧 Écoute (1–3) et regarde le diagramme. Note les deux thèmes: A ou B? C ou D?

Exemple: **1 B, ...**

4 c 💬 Regarde le diagramme et joue deux dialogues.

4 d ✏️ extra! Écris un dialogue avec deux autres thèmes.

Idées:
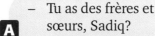 **Tu as un animal?**
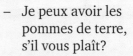 **Tu as un passe-temps?**
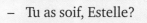 **Il y a un centre sportif?**

5 🎧 Loto: jeu 1!

Write down any four of the foods or drinks from pages 58 to 61. Listen to Kévin: tick your words when you hear them.

Loto: jeu 2! Répète le jeu!

tu aimes la viande?	
oh oui, beaucoup / non, merci	
je peux avoir le pain,	s'il vous plaît? s'il te plaît?
voilà	merci

7C Impressions de la France

- note differences between France and Britain
- understand words by looking at the endings
- write negative sentences

Voici les impressions de la classe de Sadiq après la visite à Biarritz.

A Dans ma famille en France, on a dîné à 20h30. Mais en Angleterre, dans ma famille, on dîne à 18h normalement.

B En France, les gendarmes sont armés. Je n'aime pas ça.

C En France, on écoute beaucoup de musique américaine et anglaise. Le chanteur préféré de ma correspondante, c'était Robbie Williams. Moi, je n'ai pas de CD français!

D Le cyclisme est très populaire en France. Mais on ne joue pas au cricket.

Class shared reading.

1 a 💿 Écoute et lis les textes.

Stratégies! *Understanding new words by looking at their endings*

French -**ment** often = English -**ly**, e.g.
*vrai***ment** = real**ly**

- Find an example in one of the texts; write the French and the English.

- Predict the French: probab**ly** = *probable* ❓
  general**ly** = *générale* ❓

French -**é** often = English -**ed**, e.g.
*dîn***é** = din**ed** = ate, *arriv***é** = arriv**ed**

- So can you work out:
  les gendarmes sont armés
  the police are ❓

1 b 📖 Lis les textes et réponds en anglais.

A Who has their evening meal at **a** 8.30pm **b** 6pm?

B What was this student's reaction to armed police?

C What difference between France and Britain did this student notice?

D Which sport is popular in France, and which isn't played at all?

en France,	on dîne
en Grande-Bretagne,	on écoute
	on ne joue pas

2 ✎ extra! Adapte les phrases pour la Grande-Bretagne avec *ne ... pas*.

Exemple: **1 Les gendarmes *ne* sont *pas* armés.**

1 Les gendarmes ⌃ sont ⌃ armés.
2 En Grande-Bretagne, normalement, on ⌃ dîne ⌃ très tard.
3 On ⌃ écoute ⌃ beaucoup de musique française.
4 Le handball et le cyclisme ⌃ sont ⌃ très populaires.

◀

> ♻ **Grammaire**
> To make sentences negative:
> 1 put **ne** or **n'** in front of the verb
> 2 put **pas** after the verb.

Sommaire
Sadiq en France • 7

Le dîner	**The evening meal**
bon appétit	*enjoy your meal*
tu as faim?	*are you hungry?*
tu as soif?	*are you thirsty?*
oui, j'ai faim	*yes, I'm hungry*
j'ai soif	*I'm thirsty*
j'aime...	*I like...*
tu aimes... ?	*do you like...?*
les gâteaux au chocolat	*chocolate cake*
le jus d'orange	*orange juice*
la soupe	*soup*
la viande	*meat*
l'eau *f*	*water*
les pommes de terre	*potatoes*
les carottes	*carrots*
les pâtes	*pasta*
les biscuits	*biscuits*
les frites	*chips*
oui, beaucoup	*yes, a lot*
non, pas beaucoup	*no, not much*
je préfère l'eau	*I prefer water*

Conversations	**Conversations**
je peux avoir les pâtes, s'il vous plaît?	*could I have the pasta, please? (to an adult)*
je peux avoir les pâtes, s'il te plaît?	*could I have the pasta, please? (to someone your age)*
le lait	*milk*
le pain	*bread*
le beurre	*butter*
le fromage	*cheese*
le thé	*tea*
le jambon	*ham*
voilà	*here you are*
merci	*thank you*

Impressions	**Impressions**
en France	*in France*
en Grande-Bretagne	*in Britain*
on dîne...	*people have their evening meal...*
on écoute...	*people listen...*
on ne joue pas...	*people don't play...*

Grammaire

● expressions with *avoir*:
  j'ai usually means 'I have', but note: I am 14 ***j'ai*** 14 ans, I am hungry ***j'ai*** faim, I am thirsty ***j'ai*** soif
● negative sentences
  1 put **ne** or **n'** in front of the verb
  2 put **pas** after the verb
  *on **ne** joue **pas** au cricket* they don't play cricket

1 word 2 meanings
les **pommes** – *apples*
les **pommes de terre** – *potatoes*

Stratégies!

★ saying 'please': *s'il te plaît* to young people; *s'il vous plaît* to adults

★ a conversation can cover a range of topics: be prepared!

★ understanding new words by looking at their endings: -**ment** = -**ly**; -**é** = -**ed**

8 Les médias et les stars

8A Les derniers échos

- read and listen to gossip about stars
- understand a song
- understand two uses of the past tense

les derniers échos – *the latest gossip*

Estelle et Kévin adorent les derniers échos sur les stars.

A **Hé, Estelle! Tu as entendu...?**

B **Enzo a épousé Maeva.**

C **Océane a divorcé de Bastien.**

D **Alexia Villard a eu un bébé.**

E **Valentin a rompu avec Lucie.**

F **Il sort avec Noémie Cartin.**

1 a 💿 Écoute et lis. Note les lettres dans le bon ordre.

Exemple: **1 D**

1 b 📖 Trouve les paires. Écris le français et l'anglais.

Exemple: **il a épousé – *he has married***

il a épousé...
elle sort avec...
elle a divorcé de...
elle a eu...
tu as entendu... ?
il a rompu avec...

have you heard... ?
he has broken up with...
she has had...
he has married...
she is going out with...
she has divorced...

> ◀ **Grammaire: the past tense**
>
> The past tense in French can have **two** meanings in English:
>
> *X a rompu avec Y* = X **broke up** with Y
> or X **has broken up** with Y
>
> ● What are the two meanings of this phrase? *il a bu le coca*

2 💿 extra! Écoute la radio. Réponds en anglais.

1 *How old is the singer Élodie?*
2 *Where does she live?*
3 *Why is her photo in all the magazines? (Give **two** reasons.)*

tu as entendu?		
il / elle	sort avec X	
	a	épousé X
		divorcé de X
		rompu avec X
		eu un bébé

3 a 💿 Poisson d'avril! Écoute et lis les conversations (1–3). Note les détails en anglais.

1
– Hé, tu as entendu? Le prince Harry sort avec J-Lo.
– Non! Vraiment?!
– Oui, et Britney a eu un bébé.
– Tu rigoles!
– Poisson d'avril!

2
– Tu as entendu? (...) a rompu avec (...).
– Non! Vraiment?!
– Oui, et (...) a divorcé de (...).
– Tu rigoles!
– Poisson d'avril!

3
– Tu as entendu? (...)
– Non! Vraiment?!
– Oui, et (...).
– Tu rigoles!
– Poisson d'avril!

poisson d'avril – *April Fool*

> vraiment? *really?*
> tu rigoles! *you're joking!*

3 b 💬 Joue les dialogues 1 et 2: invente les détails!

extra! **Dialogues 1, 2 et 3.**

4 💿 Écoute et lis la chanson. Mets les images dans le bon ordre.

Exemple: **lundi** – **image B**

Une semaine dans la vie d'une star

Lundi dernier à la télé:
Noé Labilier
(riche, célèbre, et beau!)
est sorti avec Salomé.

Mardi dernier à la télé:
Noé Labilier
(Oh, les belles photos!)
S'est marié avec Salomé!

refrain:
Ah! Les derniers échos!
Dans les journaux!
À la radio!
C'est rigolo! C'est rigolo!

Et mercredi, ben, Salomé
a eu un bébé.
"Il est très, très beau!"
a déclaré l'heureux Noé.

Jeudi, tu as vu? Tu as entendu?
Noé a trop bu –
ce n'était pas de l'eau!
Alors Salomé a rompu!

Vendredi, les magazines:
Une très belle piscine
chez le riche Hugo!
Salomé est en Argentine!

Et puis surprise, samedi dernier!
La belle Salomé
a quitté Hugo.
Salomé aime Noé.

8B Avez-vous des DVD?

- ask for items in a shop
- remember the silent *s* on plural nouns
- practise a dialogue in a department store

> **Kévin veut acheter le dernier DVD de Johnny Depp. Il va aux *Galeries Lafayette*, un grand magasin dans le centre de Biarritz.**

> Pardon monsieur, avez-vous des… ?

B

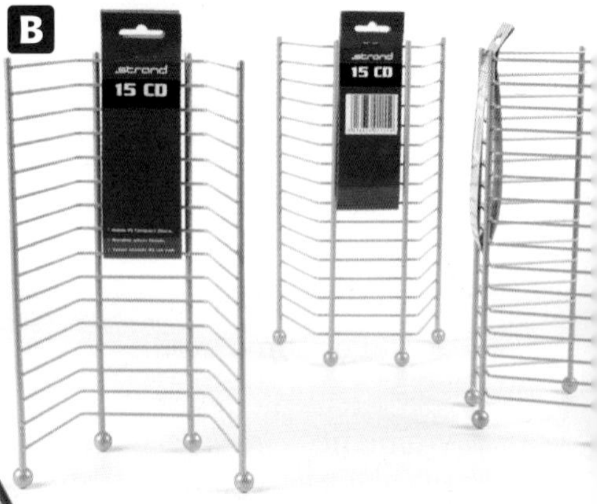

1 a 📖 Trouve les paires: mots (1–6) et photos (A–F).

Exemple: **1 A**

1. des DVD
2. des CD vierges
3. des journaux anglais
4. des agendas
5. des range-CD
6. des écouteurs

A

D

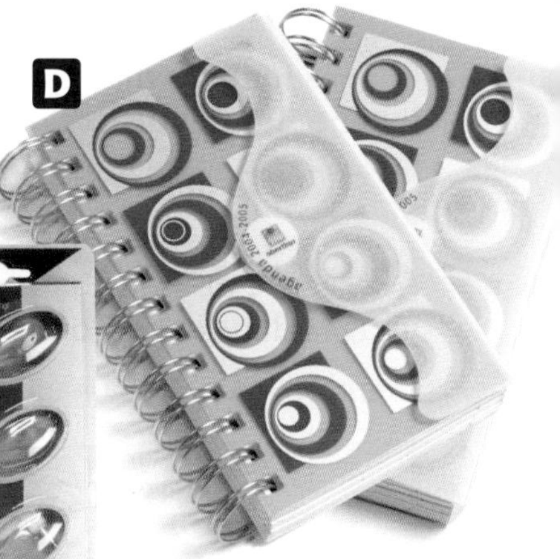

1 b ♻ Stratégies! *Silent* s

Remember? The *s* at the end of plural nouns is usually silent.

- 💿 Listen carefully: with which two nouns **is** the *s* in *des* pronounced? Can you explain why?

C

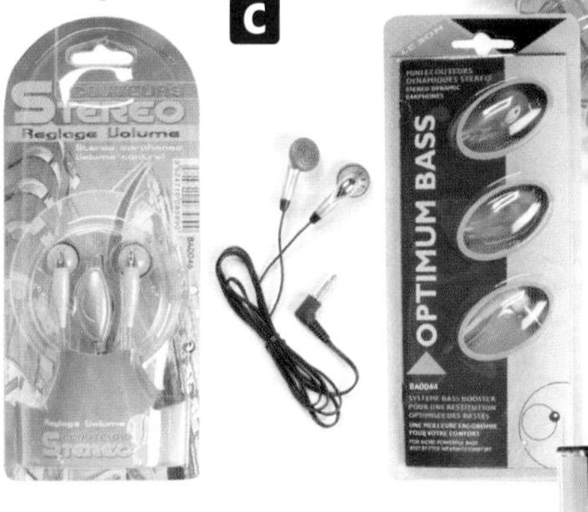

1 c 💿 Écoute et répète les questions pour A–F.

Exemple:
A Pardon madame, avez-vous des DVD?

1 d 💬 A pose une question; B identifie la photo.

Exemple: **A** Avez-vous des CD vierges?
B C'est la photo E.

E

1 e ✏ Écris les questions (1–5).

Exemple: **1** Avez-vous des écouteurs?

F

1 é s c / o r e / u u t

2 i D v / s e g / r e C

3 C a / n D / r e g

4 n g / e a / a s d

5 j u / n o x / i l g / u r a s n

2 a 💿 Écoute (1–3) et lis le dialogue. Où sont les CD vierges et les écouteurs?

Exemple: **1** en bas; là-bas

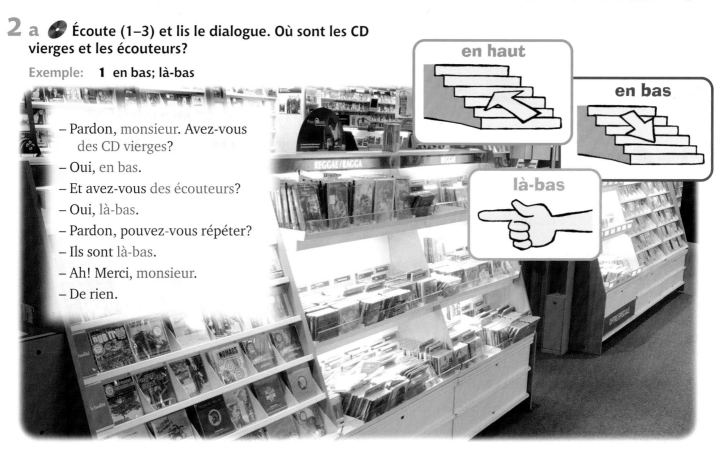

– Pardon, monsieur. Avez-vous des CD vierges?

– Oui, en bas.

– Et avez-vous des écouteurs?

– Oui, là-bas.

– Pardon, pouvez-vous répéter?

– Ils sont là-bas.

– Ah! Merci, monsieur.

– De rien.

2 b 💬 Joue les quatre dialogues A–D. Ton modèle: l'exercice 2a.

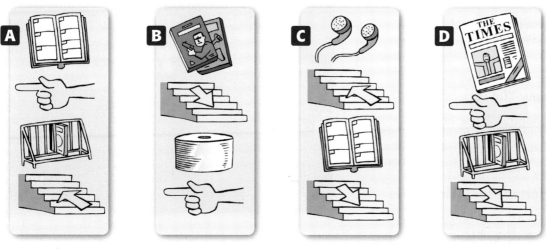

2 c ✏️ Écris *un* des dialogues A–D.

3 a 📖 extra! *How would you ask if a shop had these four items?*

`calendars`   `necklaces`   `envelopes`   `stamps`

● *Look the words up in the dictionary: remember to add an* **s**.

3 b 📖 extra! *Look up and ask for four other things in a shop.*

pardon monsieur / madame	
avez-vous des	DVD / journaux anglais range-CD / agendas écouteurs / CD vierges
oui, ils sont	en haut / en bas / là-bas
pardon, pouvez-vous répéter?	
merci	de rien

8C Dans le journal

- read a report about a fire
- work out new expressions
- present a radio report

1 a 🔘 **Écoute et lis le reportage.**

Stratégies! *Class shared reading*

- What is the article about? What are the clues that tell you?

- How many new words can you work out? *How* do you work them out?
  Example: *incendie* means 'fire' (worked out from the photo)

1 b ✏️ *Note in French and English:*

a *three time phrases* **b** *three emergency services.*

Example: **a 1 lundi soir –** *on Monday evening*

2 🔘 **Écoute les reportages (1–3). Note:**

a où est l'incendie? **b** le nombre de suspects.

Exemple: **1 a** une boucherie; **b** …

3 ♻️✏️ **À deux: vous trouvez combien d'alternatives pour "un supermarché"?**

Exemples: **1** un hôpital, **2** une école, …

8 mots = bien
15 mots = excellent!

4 ✏️ **Écris un reportage sur un incendie.**

Ton modèle: l'exercice 1a. Change les mots en rouge.

Exemple:

> Samedi soir, un incendie a ravagé un/une…

Incendie à Miremont

Lundi **soir**, un incendie **a ravagé** un supermarché.

Les pompiers sont arrivés immédiatement.

Une ambulance est arrivée dix minutes plus tard.

La police a arrêté deux suspects.

Un incendie

lundi soir, un incendie a ravagé *un supermarché*	
les pompiers sont arrivés	immédiatement
une ambulance est arrivée	*dix* minutes plus tard
la police a arrêté *deux* suspects	

5 🗨 **Tu es journaliste à la radio.**
Présente ton reportage de l'exercice 4 à la radio.
extra! **de mémoire!** (*from memory!*)

Sommaire

Les derniers échos	*The latest gossip*
tu as entendu?	*have you heard?*
elle sort avec X	*she's going out with X*
il a épousé X	*he has married X*
il a divorcé de X	*he has divorced X*
il a rompu avec X	*he has broken up with X*
elle eu un bébé	*she has had a baby*
vraiment?	*really?*
tu rigoles!	*you're joking!*

Avez-vous des DVD?	*Do you have any DVDs?*
pardon, monsieur	*excuse me* (to man)
pardon, madame	*excuse me* (to woman)
avez-vous des... ?	*do you have any... ?*
journaux anglais	*English newspapers*
range-CD	*CD racks*
agendas	*diaries*
écouteurs	*headphones*
CD vierges	*blank CDs*
DVD	*DVDs*

oui, ils sont...	*yes, they're...*
en haut	*upstairs*
en bas	*downstairs*
là-bas	*over there*
pardon, pouvez-vous répéter?	*sorry, could you repeat that?*
merci	*thank you*
de rien	*don't mention it*

Dans le journal	*In the newspaper*
lundi soir	*on Monday evening*
un incendie a ravagé un supermarché	*a fire damaged a supermarket*
les pompiers sont arrivés	*the fire brigade arrived*
une ambulance est arrivée	*an ambulance arrived*
immédiatement	*immediately*
dix minutes plus tard	*ten minutes later*
la police a arrêté deux suspects	*the police arrested two suspects*

Grammaire:

● The past tense in French can have *two* meanings in English:
  X a rompu avec Y = X **has broken up** with Y or X **broke up** with Y

Stratégies!

★ the **s** at the end of plural nouns is usually silent (unless followed by *h* or a vowel)

★ class shared reading: working out the meaning of new words

rien – *nothing*
de **rien** – *don't mention it*

Stratégies! *Preparing for your assessment*

- Look back at the *Sommaire* pages for unit 7 (p. 63) and unit 8 (p. 69). Test yourself on them (alone, or with a partner).

- Write a list of up to ten words or phrases you couldn't remember. Take your list home and fix it to the wall next to your bed. Look at the words on your list from time to time: you'll probably soon know most of them really well!

1 Écoute quatre dialogues à table (1–4) et regarde les images (A–H).
Écris deux lettres pour chaque dialogue.

Exemple: **1** B, ...

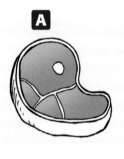

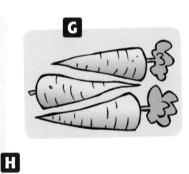

2 a Becky, une élève écossaise, dîne chez Manon, sa correspondante française.

Lis le dialogue. On parle des thèmes A–E? Écris *oui* ou *non*.

Exemple: **A** non

| A Becky's town | B a celebrity |
| C a TV programme | D a fire | E sport |

2 b Lis les cinq phrases en rouge.
Écris les cinq phrases en anglais.

Exemple: *Are you hungry, Becky? ...*

La famille	Bon appétit!
Mme Roux	Tu as faim, Becky? Tu aimes la viande?
Becky	Oh oui, beaucoup.
M. Roux	Un incendie a ravagé un supermarché en ville. Les pompiers...
Mme Roux	Tu as soif, Becky?
Becky	Non, merci... Je peux avoir les pommes de terre, s'il vous plaît?
M. Roux	Voilà, Becky.
Manon	Hé! Tu as entendu, papa? La chanteuse Zoé Souvigny sort avec un acteur américain!

3 a Recopie et complète le dialogue avec les quatre mots corrects:

| ils | pouvez | rien | vous |

3 b Joue le dialogue. Change les mots en rouge.

- Pardon, monsieur. Avez-___ ¹ des CD vierges?
- Oui, en bas.
- Pardon, ___²-vous répéter?
- ___ ³ sont en bas.
- Ah! Merci, monsieur.
- De ___ ⁴.

Pour les fans d'informatique...

Xbox live

Avec *Xbox live*, tu peux:

- jouer sur Internet
- et discuter avec tes amis.

Notre avis: Excellent pour jouer avec tes amis.

Kit Xbox Live, de Microsoft, pour Xbox, 59€ environ (un an d'abonnement incl.)

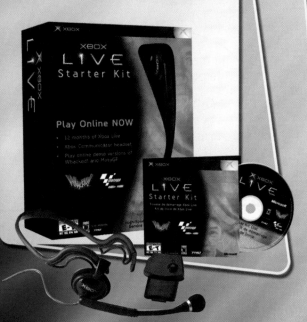

Sim City 4

Tu es maire d'une ville, et tu dois placer:

- les maisons, les magasins, les rues
- les passages de train et les installations électriques
- la police, les pompiers et les hôpitaux
- les parcs, les centres sportifs, etc.

Et ça ne doit pas coûter cher!

Ce n'est pas facile…

Notre avis: La série *Sim City* est très populaire. Et cet épisode est très beau.

Sim City 4, de EA Games, pour PC, 50€ environ

maire – *mayor*
coûter cher – *cost a lot*

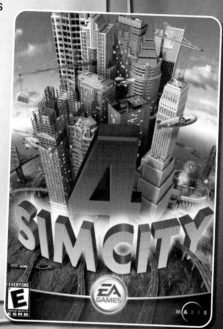

Ta star préférée sur ton PC

Tu veux voir la photo de ta star préférée sur ton PC? Pas de problème!

- Trouve une photo sur un des sites de fans.
- Sélectionne ton image et clique sur le bouton droit de ta souris.
- Dans le menu, sélectionne "Établir en tant que papier peint".

Et voilà, c'est fait!

établir en tant que papier peint
– *install as wallpaper*

1 a What does *Xbox Live* allow you to do?

1 b What do you have to do in the *Sim City 4* game? Is the game recommended?

1 c Would *you* consider buying *Xbox Live* or *Sim City 4*? Why (not)?

2 a What does the third text give you instructions to do?

2 b The third text is full of useful ICT terms! Can you find the French for… ?

1 websites	4 button
2 select	5 mouse
3 click	6 menu

9 Auditions pour la télé

9A Une vidéo personnelle

- say what you like doing
- use *j'aime* + infinitive
- sound more friendly

Il y a des interviews pour une émission de télé-réalité. 2000 candidats ont fait une vidéo. Voici quatre extraits...

1 Je m'appelle Habib. Moi, j'aime voyager avec ma famille. Je déteste faire la cuisine!

2

3 Moi, c'est Quentin. Je n'aime pas jouer aux cartes. Je préfère surfer sur Internet. Je fais souvent ça, le week-end.

Salut! Je m'appelle Karima. J'aime sortir avec mes copains. Mais je n'aime pas faire du sport.

4 Moi, c'est Amélie. J'aime beaucoup faire les magasins. Et j'adore danser aussi!

1 a 💿 **Écoute et lis. Note les noms dans le bon ordre.**

Exemple: **1 Habib**

1 b 📖 **Regarde les images (A–H). C'est qui?**

Exemple: **A Quentin**

A

B

C

D

E

F

G

H

Grammaire: *verbes + infinitif*

J'aime, je déteste, etc. are followed by the **infinitive** part of the verb (the form you find in the dictionary). This ends in **-er**, **-re** or **–ir**:

j'aime sortir I like to go out/I like going out

j'adore	sortir avec mes copains
j'aime beaucoup	voyager avec ma famille
je n'aime pas	jouer aux cartes
je déteste	surfer sur Internet
je préfère	faire du sport
	faire la cuisine
	faire les magasins
	danser

2 🖊 **Regarde la grille. Écris huit phrases avec *tes* opinions.**

Exemple: **1** Je déteste danser.

3 a 📖 **Read the descriptions. Who would you choose to go on a reality TV show, and why?**

Victor

Mathilde

> J'aime beaucoup sortir avec mes copains. Je fais souvent ça le week-end. On va à la piscine ou au cinéma. J'adore danser, aussi.
>
> Après le collège, j'aime faire les magasins en ville: c'est amusant! Le soir, j'aime surfer sur Internet, ou jouer aux cartes avec mon frère.

> Je déteste faire du vélo, je préfère jouer au tennis. Je fais ça au centre sportif, le samedi après-midi. J'aime écouter de la musique dans ma chambre.
>
> Je n'aime pas voyager avec mes parents, c'est barbant. Et faire la cuisine, c'est nul. Je ne fais jamais ça!

3 b 📖 **Relis les textes et trouve des expressions pour la grille.**

A quand? *when?*	B avec qui? *who with?*	C où? *where?*
le week-end	avec mes copains	à la...

3 c 💿 **Écoute les candidats (1–6). Note les activités.**
extra! **Note d'autres détails aussi.**

Exemple: **1** surfer (extra! avec un copain, ...)

4 💬 **Joue une interview pour l'émission de télé-réalité. Donne *tes* réponses.**

Exemple: – **Tu aimes faire quoi?**
– J'adore faire la cuisine.
– **Et tu aimes sortir?**
– Non, je préfère surfer sur Internet.
– **Et tu détestes faire quoi?**
– Je déteste faire les magasins!

> tu aimes faire quoi?
> tu aimes sortir?
> tu détestes faire quoi?

extra! Stratégies!
Sounding more friendly

Say more than the minimum when you talk about yourself. Adding details (e.g. when? where?) makes you come across as more relaxed and friendly.

9B Ma personnalité

- talk about your character
- use masculine and feminine adjectives
- make your sentences more precise

paresseux *lazy* **A**

B **heureux** *happy*

extraverti *outgoing* **C**

impertinent *cheeky* **D**

E **sportif** *sporty*

F **musicien** *musical*

G **amusant** *funny*

H **timide** *shy*

1 a 💿 **Écoute (1–6). Note les deux lettres.**

Exemple: **1 C + G**

1 b 💬 **Discute des adjectifs de personnalité. C'est une qualité positive, négative ou neutre?**

Exemple: **A** "Impertinent", c'est une qualité négative.
B Non! C'est une qualité positive!

2 💿 **Écoute (1–5). Identifie le trait de caractère.**

Exemple: **1 extraverti**

> **Formulaire pour le jury**
>
> **Sélection de candidats pour l'émission**
>
> Le candidat est-il:
>
> - paresseux? ☐
> - extraverti? ☐
> - heureux? ☐
> - musicien? ☐
> - sportif? ☐
> - timide? ☐
> - impertinent? ☐
> - amusant? ☐
>
> Notez votre opinion, s'il vous plaît.

Grammaire: *les adjectifs*

3 a 💿 *Listen. Which adjectives are pronounced differently in masculine and feminine? Discuss with your teacher.*

3 b 💿 *Listen carefully to the adjective in six sentences, and you'll be able to tell if the names below are boys' or girls' names!*

masculin (il est...)	féminin (elle est...)
paresseux	paresseuse
heureux	heureuse
sportif	sportive
extraverti	extravertie
musicien	musicienne
impertinent	impertinente
amusant	amusante
timide	timide

1 Maxence
2 Yanis
3 Rayan
4 Sakiné
5 Margaux
6 Inès

Example: **1 girl**

4 ✐ Écris une phrase pour chaque image: Il est.../Elle est...

Exemple: **1** Elle est extravertie.

5 a Stratégies! *Being more precise*

The words in red (e.g. *toujours* – always) make these descriptions more precise.

● Copy the red words and write what they mean in English.

5 b 📖 Lis les textes. C'est vrai (V) ou faux (F)?

1 Marion est parfois paresseuse.
2 Khaled est très, très sportif.
3 Maëlle est souvent très amusante.
4 Léo est extraverti.

> Ma mère déclare que je suis très impertinente et parfois paresseuse. Eh oui, c'est vrai, je suppose!

Marion

> À mon avis, je suis assez sportif et pas très musicien. Je ne suis jamais paresseux.

Khaled

> Ma sœur Maëlle est toujours heureuse, et elle est souvent très amusante.

Lena

> Mon frère est vraiment extraverti. Il adore sortir le soir. Moi, je suis toujours assez timide. Je ne sors jamais sans mes copains.

sans – *without*

Léo

il/elle est	parfois	très	impertinent	impertinente
je suis	souvent	assez	heureux	heureuse
je ne suis pas	toujours	vraiment	etc.	etc.
je ne suis jamais				

6 💬 Joue les interviews. Change les adjectifs.

Exemples:

1 A Tu es souvent timide?
B Oui, je suis souvent timide.
Je suis parfois timide.
Non, je ne suis jamais timide.

2 A Tu es très musicien(ne)?
B Oui, je suis très musicien(ne).
Je suis assez musicien(ne).
Non, je ne suis pas vraiment musicien(ne).

7 ✐ Décris ta personnalité. Écris 3–4 phrases.

Exemple: Je suis parfois assez paresseuse, mais...

8 💿 extra! Écoute et note quatre détails *en anglais* pour chaque candidat.

Exemple: **1** *called Pierre, extrovert, ...*

9C Succès!

- read a longer text
- adapt a text with your own ideas

20.45 La Maison Verte

Émission de télé-réalité. 10 personnes
A dans une maison: à vous de voter!

Star pendant quatre semaines!

En février, j'ai fait une vidéo de candidat. J'ai envoyé ma vidéo à TF1.

Dix semaines plus tard, je suis allé à Paris pour une interview. Hourra! Succès!

Joseph, la star!

La famille de Joseph regarde l'émission

B Le 23 juin, je suis entré dans la Maison Verte. C'était vraiment génial!

Il y avait neuf autres personnes. Ashraf était très amusant; Louise n'était jamais heureuse!

Le samedi, on a fait un barbecue.

C Au premier vote, Louise a dû quitter la Maison. Ouf! Pas moi!

Mais la quatrième semaine: désastre! C'était mon tour: j'ai dû quitter la Maison. C'était fantastique dans la Maison!

j'ai dû quitter – *I had to leave*

Class shared reading

This is a longer text, but it has lots of words that you've seen before. It doesn't matter if you don't understand every word. Go for it!

1 a 💿 Écoute et lis le texte A.

1 What is la Maison Verte?

2 What did candidates have to do to get on the show?

1 b 💿 Écoute et lis A et B. C'est quoi en français?

Exemple: 1 *I made* – j'ai fait

1 *I made*	**5** *it was*
2 *I sent*	**6** *there were nine other people*
3 *I went*	**7** *Ashraf was*
4 *I entered*	**8** *we had a barbecue*

1 c 💿 Écoute et lis A, B et C.

1 What were Ashraf and Louise like?

2 After which vote did Louise leave the house?

3 How long did Joseph last on the show?

1 d 🔘 Écoute un texte similaire.
Il y a une différence? Lève la main.

1 e ✏️ extra! Imagine: tu es sélectionné(e) pour une émission de télé-réalité!

Recopie la description et change les mots en rouge. Invente les détails.

Exemple: En mars, j'ai fait une vidéo de candidat. J'ai...

Sommaire

Une vidéo personnelle	A personal video	Ma personnalité	My personality
j'adore...	I love...	souvent	often
j'aime beaucoup...	I very much like...	parfois	sometimes
je n'aime pas...	I don't like...	toujours	always
je déteste...	I hate...	très	very
je préfère...	I prefer...	assez	quite
sortir avec mes copains	going out with my friends	vraiment	really
jouer aux cartes	playing cards	il est...	he is...
surfer sur Internet	surfing the internet	elle est...	she is...
voyager avec ma famille	travelling with my family	je suis...	I am...
danser	dancing	je ne suis pas...	I'm not...
faire du sport	doing sport	je ne suis jamais...	I'm never...
faire la cuisine	cooking	impertinent(e)	cheeky
faire les magasins	going round the shops	amusant(e)	funny
tu aimes faire quoi?	what do you like doing?	extraverti(e)	extrovert, outgoing
tu aimes sortir?	do you like going out?	musicien(ne)	musical
tu détestes faire quoi?	what do you hate doing?	heureux, heureuse	happy
		paresseux, paresseuse	lazy
		sportif, sportive	sporty
		timide	shy

Grammaire:
- *J'aime, je déteste*, etc. are followed by the **infinitive** part of the verb:
  j'aime sortir I like to go out/I like going out
- masculine and feminine adjectives
  - add **-e** to masculine adjectives to make them feminine (unless they end in **-e** already)
  - note some special cases: *elle est heureuse, sportive, musicienne*

Stratégies!

★ extra! sounding more friendly by saying more than the minimum

★ making your sentences more precise by using *parfois, souvent, assez, très, vraiment, jamais*

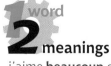
1 word 2 meanings

j'aime **beaucoup** danser – *I like dancing **very much***
il y a **beaucoup** de collines – *there are **a lot** of hills*

10 Kévin en Angleterre

10A Une soirée

- make conversation when you meet new people at a party
- give more than one-word answers

En février, Sadiq et d'autres élèves de York sont allés à Biarritz.

Ce matin, les élèves français arrivent à York. On fait une grande soirée ce soir...

A Moi, je m'appelle Rachel. Et toi? Comment t'appelles-tu?

Je m'appelle Justine.

les adresses e-mail
@ = arobase
.fr = point F R

1 💿 **Écoute et lis. Réponds en anglais.**

1 *Where did Sadiq go in February?*

2 *Who is arriving in York this morning?*

3 *What is happening this evening?*

2 a 💿 **Regarde l'image. Écoute et lis les conversations à la soirée. Trouve et écris les questions en français.**

1 *What's your email address?*

2 *Would you like some crisps?*

3 *Do you support a football team?*

4 *What sort of music do you like?*

2 b 💿 **Écoute. Note A–E dans le bon ordre.**

2 c 🗨 **Joue les dialogues A–E.**

2 d 💿 **Écoute (1–4). On offre quoi? Note les bons mots.**

Exemple: **1 un sandwich, du coca**

de la pizza	du coca
des chips	du jus d'orange
un biscuit	de l'eau minérale
un sandwich	de la limonade

2 e ✏ **Imagine une longue conversation entre deux célébrités!**

Écris la conversation: change les mots en rouge des dialogues A–E.

comment t'appelles-tu?	je m'appelle *Justine*
tu aimes quelle sorte de musique?	j'aime la musique de *Dr Dre*
	je préfère *Air*
c'est quoi, ton adresse e-mail?	*Lucas.Martin@laposte.net*
tu supportes une équipe de football?	oui, je supporte *Toulouse FC*
	non, je n'aime pas le football
	je préfère *le tennis*
tu veux *des chips / du coca*?	oui, je veux bien / non, merci

3 a Stratégies! *Making conversation*

You're now going to practise making conversation at a party. Try to keep the conversation going – don't just give one-word answers!

Example:

> Tu aimes la musique de Kylie?

✗ Non.

> Non, je préfère la musique de…

✓

extra! Prepare three extra questions you could ask to keep the conversation going, e.g. *Tu aimes les séries?*

3 b ✏ Chaque élève écrit une carte. Invente les infos.

Exemple:

Pierre ←	prénom féminin/masculin
Kylie Minogue ←	chanteur/chanteuse/groupe
Marianne@wanadoo.fr ←	adresse e-mail
l'Olympique de Marseille ←	équipe de football
un biscuit; du café ←	1 chose à manger; 1 chose à boire

3 c 💬 Le/La prof distribue les cartes.

Imagine: il y a une soirée.
Tu as l'identité sur ta carte.

Joue les conversations avec ton/ta partenaire.

Ton modèle: l'exercice 1.

Exemple:

> Moi, je m'appelle Pierre. Et toi? …

- talk about activities on a trip
- revise the past and future tenses
- check your work for mistakes

A

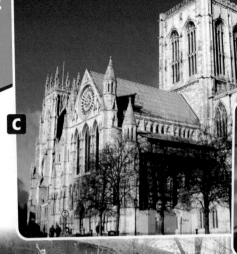

C

D

B

E

1 Écoute et lis (1–5). Trouve les paires: phrases 1–5 et photos A–E.

Exemple: **1 E**

1 En route pour York, on est allé à Londres. On a vu *Big Ben*.
2 On a fait un tour sur le *London Eye*. C'était génial!
3 À York, on est allé en ville: on est allé au marché.
4 On a fait un pique-nique près de la cathédrale.
5 Mercredi, on est allé à la mer. C'était amusant.

2 a Écoute (1–7). C'est quelle photo (a–g)?

Exemple: **1 b**

a

b

c

d

e

2 b Écris une phrase pour chaque photo (a–g).

Exemple: **A On est allé à la mer.**

f

g

| on a fait | une soirée | un barbecue | un pique-nique |
| on est allé | au marché | à la mer | dans un château | en ville |

3 a 💿 Écoute et lis le dialogue.

Père:	Allô, c'est papa. Ça va?
Kévin:	Oui, ça va bien. La famille est super! Lundi, on a fait un barbecue.
Père:	C'était bien?
Kévin:	Oui, c'était génial! Et hier, on est allé en ville.
Père:	Bon. Alors, à samedi, Kévin!
Kévin:	À samedi!

3 b 💿 Écoute cinq dialogues similaires.
Note les lettres A–F (*deux pour chaque dialogue*).

Exemple: **1 B, …**

3 c 💬 Joue et adapte le dialogue.

> ♻️ **Grammaire: past and future**
>
> | 1 | past | *on **a** fait (une soirée)* we had (a party) |
> |---|---|---|
> | | | *on **est** allé* we went |
> | 2 | future | *on **va** aller* we're going to go |

4 📖 Read the postcard.

1 *What have Kévin and the group done already?*
2 *What are they going to do on Saturday?*

lundi, *hier,*	on a fait	un pique-nique / un barbecue une soirée
	on est allé	dans un château / au marché à la mer / en ville
c'était	génial / amusant / bien	
lundi,	on va aller	dans un château

Salut, Rémi!

Je suis à York. C'est fantastique!

Lundi, on a fait un pique-nique dans un grand parc, puis on a fait du bowling. C'était vraiment amusant! Hier, on est allé à la mer.

Samedi, on va aller dans un château.

A+

Kévin

5 ✏️ Describe a trip you have made.

● *Collect 3–4 photos.*
● *Write a caption for each, saying what you did and giving your opinion.*

extra! *5–6 photos + captions.*

Stratégies! *Checking for mistakes*

Ask your partner to check the verbs in your work.

10C Merci beaucoup

- say thank you after a visit
- say what you enjoyed

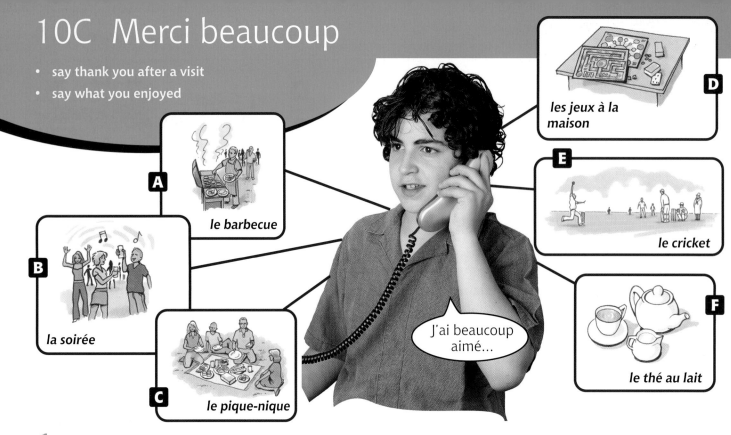

A *le barbecue*

B *la soirée*

C *le pique-nique*

D *les jeux à la maison*

E *le cricket*

F *le thé au lait*

J'ai beaucoup aimé...

1 a 💿 Écoute et lis. Note les lettres A–F dans le bon ordre.

1 b 💬 Joue six petits dialogues.

Exemple: **A** J'ai beaucoup aimé le barbecue.
B Moi aussi, c'était le top./
Moi, non. C'était nul!

2 a 💿 Écoute et lis le dialogue. ▶

2 b 💬 Joue et adapte le dialogue.

> **Idées:**
>
> le match de foot   le musée
> les jeux à la maison   le bowling
> la patinoire   le karting

extra! **Ajoute d'autres idées!**

2 c Écris un dialogue similaire.

Exemple: – **Allô.**
– **Allô, c'est Nick.**

3 💿 Listen (1–4). Note in English the things the people liked (two per dialogue).

Exemple: **1 the games in the house, ...**

Sadiq:	Allô.
Kévin:	Allô, c'est Kévin.
Sadiq:	Ah, salut Kévin. Ça va?
Kévin:	Oui, ça va bien. C'était super à York, Sadiq!
Sadiq:	Oui, c'était génial!
Kévin:	Merci pour tout! J'ai beaucoup aimé le pique-nique.
Sadiq:	Moi aussi, c'était le top! Et j'ai beaucoup aimé la soirée.
Kévin:	Bonjour à ta famille. Salut!
Sadiq:	Au revoir, Kévin!

allô, c'est Kévin	j'ai beaucoup aimé...
ça va?	les jeux à la maison
oui, ça va bien	le cricket
c'était super à York	le thé au lait
c'est bien	la soirée
merci pour tout	le barbecue
bonjour à ta famille	le pique-nique

Une soirée / A party

Une soirée	A party
comment t'appelles-tu?	*what's your name?*
je m'appelle Justine	*I'm called Justine*
tu aimes quelle sorte de musique?	*what kind of music do you like?*
j'aime la musique de Dr Dre	*I like Dr Dre's music*
je préfère Air	*I prefer Air*
c'est quoi, ton adresse e-mail?	*what's your e-mail address?*
c'est... [arobase... point...]	*it's ... [at... dot...]*
tu supportes une équipe de football?	*do you support a football team?*
oui, je supporte Toulouse FC	*yes, I support Toulouse FC*
non, je n'aime pas le football	*no, I don't like football*
je préfère le tennis	*I prefer tennis*
tu veux des chips/du coca?	*would you like some crisps?/some cola?*
oui, je veux bien/non, merci	*yes please/no thanks*

C'était génial! / It was brilliant!

C'était génial!	It was brilliant!
lundi	*on Monday*
hier	*yesterday*
on a fait…	*we had…*
un pique-nique	*a picnic*
un barbecue	*a barbecue*
une soirée	*a party*
on est allé…	*we went…*
dans un château	*to a castle*
au marché	*to the market*
à la mer	*to the seaside*
en ville	*into town*
c'était…	*it was…*
génial	*brilliant*
amusant	*fun*
bien	*good*
on va aller…	*we're going to go…*
dans un château	*to a castle*

Merci beaucoup / Thanks a lot

Merci beaucoup	Thanks a lot
allô	*hello* (on the phone)
c'est Kévin	*it's Kévin*
ça va?	*are you well?*
oui, ça va bien	*yes, I'm fine*
c'était super à York	*it was super in York*
j'ai beaucoup aimé…	*I really liked…*
les jeux à la maison	*the games in the house*
le cricket	*the cricket*
le thé au lait	*the tea with milk*
la soirée	*the party*
le barbecue	*the barbecue*
le pique-nique	*the picnic*
c'était le top	*it was brilliant*
merci pour tout	*thanks for everything*
bonjour à ta famille	*say hello to your family for me*

Grammaire: past and future

1	past	*on **a** fait (une soirée, etc.)* we had (a party, etc.)
		*on **est** allé* we went
2	future	*on **va** aller* we're going to go

Stratégies!

★ keeping a conversation going: don't just give one-word answers

★ checking your work for mistakes

1 word 2 meanings

ça va **bien** – *I'm **fine***

c'était **bien** – *it was **good***

Stratégies! *Preparing for your assessment*

- Look back at the *Sommaire* pages for unit 9 (p. 77) and unit 10 (p. 83). Test yourself, and then pick out eight words or phrases you find difficult.

- Write these in English, then write the first letters of the French words. Leave a gap for each missing letter, for example:

  I like cooking – j′ _ _ _ _ _ _   f _ _ _ _ _   l _   c _ _ _ _ _ _ _ _ _

  Come back later and try to fill in the gaps from memory.

1 a 📖 Lis les questions et les réponses. Trouve les paires.

Exemple: **1 e**

1 Comment t'appelles-tu?

2 Tu aimes faire quoi, le week-end?

a Non, je suis assez timide.

b J'aime sortir avec mes copains.

3 Tu détestes faire quoi?

4 Tu es extraverti(e)?

c Oui, je supporte Paris Saint-Germain.

d C'est mfl@tiscali.fr

5 Tu supportes une équipe de football?

6 C'est quoi, ton adresse e-mail?

e Je m'appelle Marc.

f Je déteste faire la cuisine.

1 b 💬 Joue le dialogue (six questions et réponses). Donne *tes* réponses.

Exemple: **A** Tu supportes une équipe de football?
           B Non, je n'aime pas le football.

2 a 💿 Écoute la description de la semaine dernière (lundi ➝ dimanche).

Note les images A–G dans le bon ordre.

Exemple: **E, ...**

2 b ✏️ Écris une phrase pour chaque image (A–G).

Exemple: **A On est allé en ville.**

on est allé... / on a fait...

Les voyages scolaires

Coucou! Le mois prochain, je vais aller passer une semaine à Bolton en Angleterre avec ma classe. C'est mon premier voyage scolaire, alors je suis anxieuse... Vous avez fait des voyages intéressants? Si oui, écrivez-moi! Merci.

Caroline, 13 ans

Coucou, Caro

Moi, l'année dernière, je suis allé en Italie avec le collège. Nous avons voyagé en car et nous sommes allés à Rome. J'ai adoré! Nous avons logé dans des familles italiennes très sympas.

Nous avons visité le Colisée, le Forum Romain, le musée du Capitole, le Panthéon, le Vatican et la Basilique Saint-Pierre. C'était très intéressant. Nous avons pique-niqué dans les jardins du Capitole.

Samir

Salut,

Les voyages scolaires, je trouve ça bien. L'année dernière, nous sommes allés en République Tchèque avec le collège. Nous avons visité Prague. C'était très intéressant.

Nous avons aussi visité les grottes de Macocha. Dans ces grottes, il y a des rivières avec des stalactites et des stalagmites. C'était hyper beau!

Cette année, mon frère va aller à Canterbury en Angleterre. Il va loger en auberge de jeunesse.

Bon voyage, Caro!

Ophélie

auberge de jeunesse – *youth hostel*

Caroline,

Moi aussi, je vais faire mon premier voyage scolaire cette année, en mars. Nous faisons un échange avec une école allemande et je vais aller près de Stuttgart. On va voyager en train. On va visiter la ville de Stuttgart, et on va aller au bowling et à la patinoire.

Je te souhaite un bon séjour en Angleterre!

Adrien

---

1 For each picture (A–D), note the answers to the following questions:

1 who?   **3** where?

2 what?   **4** when? (past or future?)

Exemple:
    1 Adrien
    2 skating
    3 Stuttgart in Germany
    4 in March (future)

2 Choose one of the texts and write a summary in English.

11 Des disputes

11A C'est archinul!

- argue about a range of topics
- express your opinion with feeling
- understand adjectives ending in *-ant*

La Coupe du monde

La boxe

Le gangsta rap

Tu aimes... ?

A le shopping **B** la politique **C** la Coupe du monde

D la boxe **E** la télé-réalité **F** le gangsta rap

1 a 🔘 Écoute (1–6). Note l'ordre des thèmes A–F.

Exemple: **1 C**

1 b 🔘 Écoute et note l'opinion (a–h).

Exemple: **1 d**

> **a** C'est amusant.
> **b** C'est barbant.
> **c** C'est intéressant.
> **d** C'est pénible!
> **e** C'est nul!
> **f** C'est archinul!
> **g** C'est génial!
> **h** C'est vraiment top!

pénible – *a pain*

1 c Stratégies! *Speaking with feeling*

When you give an opinion, say it with feeling!

- Your teacher will say comments a–h.
  Imitate the way he/she says them.
  Exaggerate as much as you like!

2 a 📖 C'est logique: oui ou non? Si non, écris une phrase logique.

Exemple: **1** Non. ➞ J'aime la Coupe du monde. C'est génial.

1 J'aime la Coupe du monde. C'est pénible.

2 Je déteste la boxe. C'est barbant.

3 J'aime la télé-réalité. C'est nul.

4 J'aime la politique. C'est intéressant.

5 Je déteste le shopping. C'est génial.

2 b Stratégies!

Adjectives ending in -ant

Adjectives ending in **-ant** often end **-ing** in English, e.g. *amusant* = amus**ing** (fun).

- What are these in English?
  1 *intéressant*
  2 *barbant*
  3 *terrifiant*

3 Écoute et lis, puis joue les deux dialogues.

Dialogue 1

A	Tu aimes le shopping?
B	Non! Moi, je déteste ça!
A	Quoi?? Le shopping, c'est génial!
B	Tu rigoles? C'est pénible, le shopping!
A	Mais non!! C'est vraiment top!

Dialogue 2

B	Tu aimes le gangsta rap?
A	Oui! J'adore ça.
B	Quoi?? Le gangsta rap, c'est barbant!
A	Tu rigoles?? C'est amusant, le gangsta rap!
B	Mais non! C'est archinul!!

4 Écoute les dialogues (1–5). C'est quel thème A–F (à la page 86)?
Exemple: **1 E**

extra! **Note aussi les opinions.** Exemple: **1 E** barbant, amusant, ...

tu aimes... ?		oui,	c'est	amusant / intéressant
le shopping / le gangsta rap				génial / vraiment top
la politique / la boxe			j'adore ça	
la télé-réalité		non,	c'est	barbant / pénible / nul / archinul
la Coupe du monde			je déteste ça	
quoi??	tu rigoles??		mais non!!	

5 a Écris trois dialogues. Change A, B et C.

– Moi, j'aime **A** la boxe.
– Tu rigoles? C'est **B** barbant!
– Mais non! **A** La boxe, c'est **C** génial!

A le shopping, le gangsta rap, la politique, la télé-réalité, la boxe, la Coupe du monde

B barbant, pénible, nul, archinul

C amusant, intéressant, génial, vraiment top

5 b Joue trois autres dialogues, avec expression!

extra! **Discute de deux autres thèmes, par exemple 1 les graffitis 2 le collège.**

6 Lis le texte. Réponds en anglais.

1 *What sort of music does Stéphanie like?*
2 *What sports does she do?*
3 *What events does she like watching on TV?*
4 *Which activity doesn't she like?*
5 *What does she do in the evenings?*

J'aime beaucoup le gangsta rap, mais parfois je préfère la musique classique.

J'aime beaucoup le sport. J'adore faire du kayak, et j'aime jouer au tennis et au handball. J'adore regarder la Coupe du monde et les Jeux olympiques à la télé.

Par contre, je déteste la boxe. À mon avis, c'est une activité barbare.

Le soir, je téléphone à mes copines.

Stéphanie

11B Les zoos

- discuss the pros and cons of zoos
- use *c'est* and *ce n'est pas*
- reuse language you know

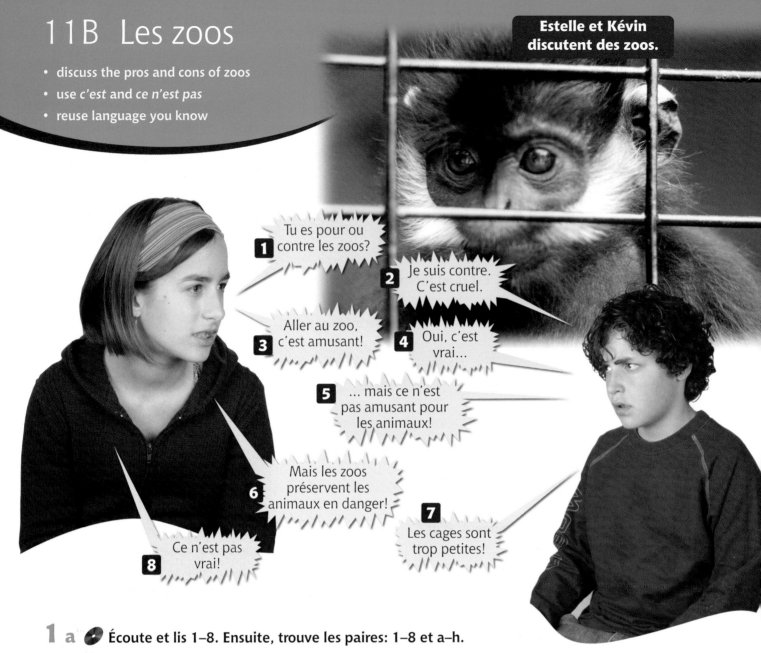

Estelle et Kévin discutent des zoos.

1 Tu es pour ou contre les zoos?

2 Je suis contre. C'est cruel.

3 Aller au zoo, c'est amusant!

4 Oui, c'est vrai...

5 ... mais ce n'est pas amusant pour les animaux!

6 Mais les zoos préservent les animaux en danger!

7 Les cages sont trop petites!

8 Ce n'est pas vrai!

1 a 💿 Écoute et lis 1–8. Ensuite, trouve les paires: 1–8 et a–h.

Exemple: **1 g**

a *The cages are too small.*
b *But zoos protect endangered animals.*
c *That's not true.*
d *Going to the zoo is fun.*
e *... but it's no fun for the animals.*
f *I'm against. It's cruel.*
g *Are you for or against zoos?*
h *Yes, that's true...*

1 b ✏️ Écris les phrases 2, 3, 5, 6 et 7 dans deux listes:

Pour les zoos	Contre les zoos
	Je suis contre. C'est cruel.

2 Grammaire: *c'est* it is, *ce n'est pas* it isn't

c'est vrai = **it's** true   **ce n'est pas** vrai = **it isn't** true

- *c'est* amusant = it's fun
- _❓_ cruel = it's cruel
- _❓_ amusant = it isn't fun
- _❓_ cruel = it isn't cruel

3 🔵 Écoute, puis joue les deux dialogues.

Dialogue 1

Grégory	Tu es pour ou contre les zoos?
Alice	Moi, je suis contre.
Grégory	Pourquoi?
Alice	C'est cruel!
Grégory	Mais non! Ce n'est pas vrai! Les zoos préservent les animaux en danger.

Dialogue 2

Talal	Tu es pour ou contre les zoos?
Solène	Moi, je suis pour.
Talal	Pourquoi?
Solène	Aller au zoo, c'est amusant.
Talal	Oui, c'est vrai, mais les cages sont trop petites.

je suis / tu es	pour ou contre	les zoos?
pourquoi?	c'est cruel	
	ce n'est pas amusant pour les animaux	
	les cages sont trop petites	
	les zoos préservent les animaux en danger	
	aller au zoo, c'est amusant	
c'est vrai	ce n'est pas vrai	

4 a 💬 Et *tes* opinions? Discute des zoos avec ton/ta partenaire.

Exemple: **A** Tu es pour ou contre les zoos?
B Je suis pour / contre.
A Pourquoi?
B *(ton opinion)*
A Oui, c'est vrai, / Non, ce n'est pas vrai, + *(ton opinion)*.

Opinions:
c'est cruel
ce n'est pas amusant pour les animaux
c'est amusant pour les enfants
les zoos préservent les animaux en danger

4 b 💬 extra! Discute aussi de ces thèmes.

Ton modèle: l'exercice 4a.

Stratégies!

Reusing language you know

Use expressions you've learnt so far in this unit, e.g.

Je suis contre la chasse. C'est cruel.

5 🔵 Écoute les discussions 1–4. Identifie le thème (A–E).

A les zoos **B** la boxe **C** le collège
D la télé **E** le gangsta rap

Les cirques

La chasse

L'élevage en batterie

- read a longer text
- adapt model sentences from a text

Les populations animales

🐾 Il existe 5 000 à 7 500 tigres en liberté. 3 000 de ces tigres en liberté se trouvent en Inde. En plus, il y a 10 000 tigres en captivité.

🐾 Les tigres sont des carnivores. Un tigre mange trois tonnes de viande par an.

🐾 Il existe entre 35 000 et 50 000 éléphants en liberté, estime la WWF. Le nombre d'éléphants d'Asie représente environ 10% du nombre d'éléphants d'Afrique.

🐾 Le nombre de rhinocéros noirs a diminué de 65 000 animaux dans les années 1970 à 2 400 animaux en 1995.

Maintenant, il existe 3 600 rhinocéros noirs. En plus, il existe environ 11 000 rhinocéros blancs.

🐾 22 000 ours polaires habitent les territoires arctiques (il n'existe pas d'ours polaire au pôle Sud!). 60% des ours polaires sont au Canada.

🐾 Les pingouins habitent au pôle Sud, pas au pôle Nord!

> en liberté – *in the wild*
> maintenant – *now*
> environ – *about*

1 a 💿 **Écoute et lis l'article. Explique les chiffres a–f en anglais.**

Exemple:　**a** *the number of tigers in the wild*

a 5 000–7 500　　**d** 11 000

b 10 000　　　　　**e** 35 000–50 000

c 3 600　　　　　　**f** 22 000

1 b 📖 **Note dix mots français qui ressemblent à des mots anglais. extra! 15 mots!**

Exemple:　**existe** – *exist*, **tigres** – *tigers*, …

1 c 📖 **Note in English three interesting facts from the texts.**

2 🖊 *Use the internet to find similar statistics about any other type of animal. Then write your findings in French.*

Stratégies!

Using model sentences from a text

To say what *you* want to say, you can often adapt sentences from reading texts, e.g.

- *Il existe 5 000–7 500 tigres en liberté.* There are 5,000–7,500 tigers in the wild.

→ *Il existe 1 600 pandas géants en liberté.*

C'est archinul! — *It's complete rubbish!*

tu aimes... ?	*do you like... ?*
le shopping	*shopping*
le gangsta rap	*gangsta rap*
la politique	*politics*
la télé-réalité	*reality TV*
la boxe	*boxing*
la Coupe du monde	*the World Cup*
oui, c'est...	*yes, it's...*
amusant	*fun*
intéressant	*interesting*
génial	*great*
vraiment top	*really great*

non, c'est...	*no, it's...*
barbant	*boring*
pénible	*a pain*
nul	*rubbish*
archinul	*complete rubbish*
j'adore ça	*I love it*
moi, je déteste ça	*I hate it*
quoi??	*what??*
tu rigoles?	*are you joking?*
mais non!	*of course not!*

Les zoos — *Zoos*

je suis...	*I am...*
tu es... ?	*are you... ?*
pour ou contre les zoos	*for or against zoos*
pourquoi?	*why?*
c'est cruel	*it's cruel*
ce n'est pas amusant pour les animaux	*it's no fun for the animals*
les cages sont trop petites	*the cages are too small*
les zoos préservent les animaux en danger	*zoos conserve endangered animals*
aller au zoo, c'est amusant	*going to the zoo is fun*
c'est vrai	*that's true*
ce n'est pas vrai	*that isn't true*

Grammaire:

● **c'est** it is, **ce n'est pas** it isn't: *c'est vrai* it's true, *ce n'est pas vrai* it isn't true

Stratégies!

★ speaking with feeling when you have a strong opinion about something

★ working out the meaning of new words by applying your knowledge of French (e.g. adjectives that end in **-ant** in French often end in **-ing** in English)

★ extra! reusing language you know

★ using model sentences from a reading text

1 word 2 meanings

il y a **trop** de violence à la télé – *there's **too much** violence on TV*
les cages sont **trop** petites – *the cages are **too** small*

12 Une réception à Paris

12A À la réception

- have a conversation covering different topics
- keep a conversation going

1 📖 Sadiq va à Paris. Pourquoi? Lis le texte et explique en anglais. ▶

2 a 📖 Trouve et écris les paires: questions (1–5) et réponses (A–E).

> Des élèves britanniques, italiens, espagnols, etc. ont inventé des pièces de théâtre en français.
>
> 20 élèves ont gagné deux jours à Paris avec une réception dans un grand hôtel. Et Sadiq a gagné!

une pièce de théâtre – *a play*
gagné – *won*

1 Tu as des frères et sœurs?
◀◀ p. 13

2 Tu aimes les séries à la télé?
◀◀ p. 21

3 Tu as fait quoi le week-end dernier?
◀◀ pp. 31 et 83

4 C'est qui, ta star préférée? Pourquoi?
◀◀ p. 39

5 Tu es pour ou contre les zoos?
◀◀ p. 91

A Samedi, on a fait une excursion à Newcastle et dimanche, on a regardé un film.

B Non, je préfère les émissions de sport.

C Ma star préférée, c'est Dr Dre, parce qu'il est très original.

D Je suis contre, parce que les cages sont trop petites. C'est cruel!

E Non, je suis enfant unique.

2 b 🔘 Écoute et vérifie.

2 c 💬 A dit une réponse; B identifie la question.

Exemple: **A** "Non, je préfère les émissions de sport."
B "Tu aimes les séries à la télé?"
A Oui, c'est juste!

3 🔘 extra! Écoute (1–5). Note les réponses en anglais.

Exemple: **1** *Yes, I have a brother and a sister.*

tu as des frères et sœurs?	oui, j'ai un frère / une sœur		non, je suis enfant unique
tu aimes les *séries* à la télé?	non, je préfère les *émissions de sport*		
tu as fait quoi *le week-end* dernier?	samedi, dimanche,	on a	regardé *un film* / fait une excursion à *Newcastle*
c'est qui, ta star préférée? pourquoi?	ma star préférée, c'est…, parce qu'*il est très original*		
tu es pour ou contre *les zoos*?	je suis pour / contre		

4 a ✏️ Écris *tes* réponses aux questions 1–5.

Exemple: **1** J'ai une sœur. Je n'ai pas de frère.

4 b 💬 Pose les questions 1–5 à ton/ta partenaire dans un ordre différent. Donne *tes* réponses à ton/ta partenaire.

Stratégies! *Returning the question*

A good tip for keeping a conversation going is to return the question. You can simply say:

Et toi? What about you?

5 💬 Imagine: tu es à la réception. Joue une conversation avec un(e) autre invité(e). Au signal de ton/ta prof, change de partenaire.

◀ Stratégies! **Using the Sommaire *pages***

Look back at the *Sommaire* pages to remind yourself of words you need. (The page numbers are given next to the questions.)

Exemple: **A** Tu aimes les séries à la télé?
B Oui, j'aime beaucoup les séries. **Et toi?**
A Non, je préfère les émissions de télé-réalité.

Idée! Organisez une vraie soirée en classe!

12B La pièce de théâtre

- read and listen to Sadiq's play
- act out the play

Sadiq's winning play is on page 95. It's a spoof whodunnit murder mystery.

1 a 💿 Écoute et lis la pièce de théâtre de Sadiq. Note le bon ordre des images (A–F).

1 b 📖 Explain in English.

1 Who was the victim?

2 Who was the murderer?

3 How did Sholmes know who the murderer was?

4 What was the murderer's motive?

1 c 📖 C'est qui? Écris le bon nom.

Sholmes **Charlotte** **Sophie** **Jacques**

1 L'assassin, c'est...

2 Elle dîne avec Jacques ce soir. C'est...

3 La victime, c'est...

4 Le détective, c'est...

2 💬 En groupes, jouez la pièce de théâtre. ▶

Stratégies! *Acting out a play*

Turn it into a radio play (with a narrator and sound effects), or act it out in class.

- Work in groups, and take a role each.
- Practise your lines.
  - Ask for help with any words you're not sure how to pronounce.
  - Remember, the play is a spoof, so your acting can be really over the top!
- Practise the play as a group, and act it out when you're ready.

Une énigme pour Herlock Sholmes – par Sadiq Akbar

Dans un restaurant. Il y a deux tables.
À la table 1, le détective Herlock Sholmes et une amie, Sophie.
À la table 2, deux amants: Jacques et Charlotte.

Jacques	Ah, Charlotte. Je t'aime!
Charlotte	Ah, Jacques! Tu es fantastique!
Sholmes	Mmm! La soupe est délicieuse!
Sophie	Je n'aime pas la soupe, moi.
Jacques	Un moment, chérie. Je vais aux toilettes.
Charlotte	Et moi, je vais appeler un taxi.

(Jacques et Charlotte quittent la salle.)

Sophie	Aïe! J'ai mal à l'estomac!!
Sholmes	Ah?
Sophie	Je dois aller aux toilettes!

(Sophie quitte la salle. Dix secondes plus tard: PAN!! PAN!! Il y a deux coups de revolver et un cri terrible. Jacques, les mains sur l'estomac, revient.)

Jacques	Aaaaaaaaah!!!!!!
Sholmes	Oh là là!!

(Jacques meurt. Charlotte revient; Sophie revient aussi.)

Charlotte	Jacques! Jacques! Mon chéri!
Sholmes	Sophie, tu as vu l'assassin?
Sophie	Non. Je suis allée aux toilettes des femmes. J'ai vomi.
Sholmes	Et vous, madame?
Charlotte	Non. Moi, j'ai appelé un taxi.
Sholmes	Excusez-moi. Je vais regarder dans les toilettes des hommes.

(Herlock Sholmes quitte la salle. Dix secondes plus tard, il revient.)

Sholmes	Ce portable était dans les toilettes des hommes.
Charlotte	Ce n'est pas *mon* portable.
Sophie	Ce n'est pas *mon* portable.

(Soudain, le portable sonne: Tu – lu – lulu – lulu – lu!)

Sholmes	Allô? ... Sophie, c'est pour toi.
Sophie	Mais...
Sholmes	Et moi, j'ai la solution. C'est *ton* portable, Sophie. Toi, tu es allée dans les toilettes des hommes, et l'assassin, c'est toi!
Sophie	Oui, c'est vrai. C'est moi.
Charlotte	Vous? Mais... pourquoi?
Sophie	Jacques était *mon* amant. Et puis, j'ai vu Jacques avec vous – le monstre!
Charlotte	Assassin!!

deux amants – *two lovers*
chéri(e) – *darling*
quittent – *leave*
revient – *comes back*
meurt – *dies*
femmes – *women*
hommes – *men*

- enjoy using the French you have learnt

A Quatre illusions d'optique

1 Le cercle A est plus grand que le cercle B: vrai ou faux?

A

B

2 C'est quoi?

3 C'est quoi?

4 C'est quoi?

B Deux blagues

1

Docteur, je suis persuadé que je suis invisible.

Qui parle?

2 Jules a un accident. Il va chez le docteur.

Jules: Je peux jouer au football?

Docteur: Oui.

Jules: Je peux faire du vélo?

Docteur: Oui, oui!

Jules: Certain?

Docteur: Certain!

Jules: Ça, c'est cool! Avant l'accident, je ne savais pas faire du vélo!

je peux...? – *can I...?*
avant – *before*
je ne savais pas – *I couldn't*

C Quelle est l'opinion de Sadiq sur Estelle?

- Fais les maths sur une calculatrice:

$$31100$$
$$+ \ 6638$$
_____

- Tourne la calculatrice à l'envers – et voilà son opinion!

Une calculatrice

31100

D Spot the clue!

Four pupils are showing off about their holidays. Read and listen to the text and look at the pictures: can you tell who is making it all up?

"En août, j'ai passé un week-end super à Paris," a dit Djamel. "J'ai vu la tour Eiffel. C'était fantastique. Regarde, j'ai une photo."

"Bof, Paris... Moi, je suis allée aux États-Unis," a dit Margot. "On a visité New York, puis on a visité Disneyland. C'était génial. Regarde, j'ai aussi une photo."

"Les USA, ce n'est pas génial," a répondu Anthony. "Moi, j'ai fait un safari au Kenya, en Afrique. J'ai vu beaucoup d'animaux. J'ai beaucoup aimé les tigres. Regarde!"

"Et moi, je suis allée en Australie," a dit Sabrina. "Regarde ma photo, les kangourous sont amusants, non?"

Sommaire

À la réception	At the reception		
tu as des frères et sœurs?	*do you have any brothers and sisters?*	on a regardé un film dimanche	*we watched a film on Sunday*
oui, j'ai un frère	*yes, I have a brother*	on a fait une excursion à Leeds	*we went on a trip to Leeds*
oui, j'ai une sœur	*yes, I have a sister*	c'est qui, ta star préférée?	*who is your favourite star?*
non, je suis enfant unique	*no, I'm an only child*	ma star préférée, c'est…	*my favourite star is…*
tu aimes les séries à la télé?	*do you like series on TV?*	pourquoi?	*why?*
non, je préfère les émissions de sport	*no, I prefer sports programmes*	parce qu'il est très original	*because he's very original*
tu as fait quoi le week-end dernier?	*what did you do last weekend?*	tu es pour ou contre les zoos?	*are you for or against zoos?*
samedi	*on Saturday*	je suis pour	*I'm in favour*
		je suis contre	*I'm against*

Stratégies!

★ looking back at the *Sommaire* pages to remind yourself of words you need

★ returning the question by asking *Et toi?* – 'What about you?'

★ acting out a play

1 word 2 meanings

à Leeds – **to** *Leeds*
à la télé – **on** *TV*

Réponse D: Anthony a inventé ses vacances. Il n'y a pas de tigre en Afrique!

Stratégies! *Preparing for your assessment*

- Test yourself on the *Sommaire* pages for unit 11 (p. 91) and unit 12 (p. 97).

- Revision is most effective when you're doing something *active* (not just reading through!).

  For example, write out any four words or phrases you find hard to remember. Next to each one, write down *what* you find hard (spelling? gender? pronunciation? word order?), for example:

  > *le week-end dernier* – last weekend. I forget that *dernier* comes **after** *week-end!*

  The next day, ask your partner to test you on these four. You'll probably get them right!

1 a Écoute les discussions (1–6). Note les thèmes (A–F) dans le bon ordre.

Exemple: **1 C**

A le shopping **B** le gangsta rap **C** la Coupe du monde

D la boxe **E** la télé-réalité **F** la politique

1 b Joue, puis adapte le dialogue.

- Tu aimes la Coupe du monde?
- Non, je déteste ça!
- Quoi?? La Coupe du monde, c'est génial!
- Tu rigoles? C'est barbant!

j'adore ça   amusant
intéressant   vraiment top

pénible   nul   archinul

1 c Écris les opinions en français et en anglais.

Exemple: **1 C'est nul, la politique!** – *Politics is rubbish!*

1 C'est n*l, la p*l*t*q**!

2 La t*l*-r**l*t*, c'est g*n**l!

3 C'est p*n*bl*, le sh*pp*ng!

4 La C**p* d* m*nd*, c'est vr**m*nt top!

2 Lis le texte et réponds en anglais.

1 *What did Lisa do last Saturday?*
2 *What did she particularly like?*
3 *When was the electricity cut?*
4 *Who screamed?*
5 *Who had stood on Laetitia's foot?*

Normalement, je n'aime pas danser. Mais samedi dernier, je suis allée danser. C'était bien: j'ai beaucoup aimé la musique.

À neuf heures, soudain, on a coupé l'électricité! Il a fait noir... et puis il y a eu un cri terrible!

Finalement, on a continué à danser. Et le cri? C'était Laetitia. Son ami Nicolas lui avait marché sur le pied!

Lisa

couper – *to cut*   un cri – *a scream*
avait marché sur – *had stood on*

Super soirée

1 À la soirée d'Amélie,
On a mangé du curry
Et bu des super jus de fruits.
On a ri, on a dansé,
On a écouté des CD,
On s'est super bien amusé.

Super soirée! Merci, Amélie!

2 J'ai rencontré Alexis.
Il m'a souri et a dit:
"C'est quoi ton groupe préféré?
Tu regardes des séries?
Tu aimes la télé-réalité?
C'est important la liberté?"

Super soirée! Merci, Amélie!

3 On a parlé de musique
Et de télé et d'Afrique
Et aussi de politique.
J'ai dit: "Je suis contre les zoos!
Ce n'est vraiment pas rigolo
Pour tous ces pauvres
animaux!"

Super soirée! Merci, Amélie!

4 Il a fini son jus de fruits
Et ses carottes au curry,
Et il a dit "Moi aussi!
Je préfère les bêtes en liberté,
Surtout dans les Pyrénées!
Mais maintenant viens danser!"

Super soirée! Merci, Amélie!

on a ri – *we laughed*
il m'a souri – *he smiled at me*
rigolo – *fun*
pauvre – *poor*
les bêtes en liberté – *animals in the wild*
surtout – *especially*

1 **Find the right picture for each verse.**

2 **Answer the questions.**

1 Whose party was it?
2 What did Alexis eat?
3 What did he drink?
4 What did they listen to?
5 What four things did Alexis and the girl talk about?

3 extra! **Choose your favourite verse and learn it by heart.**

1 a 📖 **Find the matching pairs: questions and answers (1–5) and themes (A–E).** (◄◄ pp. 6–7)

Example: **1 B**

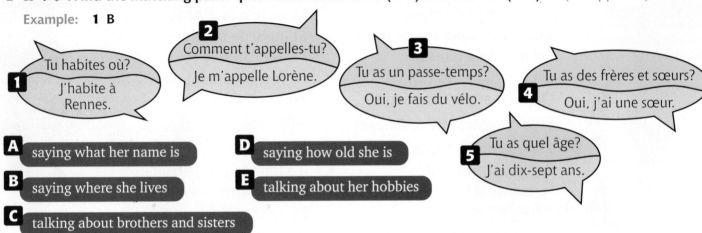

2
Comment t'appelles-tu?
Je m'appelle Lorène.

1
Tu habites où?
J'habite à Rennes.

3
Tu as un passe-temps?
Oui, je fais du vélo.

4
Tu as des frères et sœurs?
Oui, j'ai une sœur.

5
Tu as quel âge?
J'ai dix-sept ans.

A saying what her name is

B saying where she lives

C talking about brothers and sisters

D saying how old she is

E talking about her hobbies

1 b 🖊 **Look at sentences 1–5 in English. Then write sentences 1–5 in French.**

Example: **1 *Je m'appelle Nathan.***

1 *I'm called Nathan.*	**1** Je	à	Nathan.
2 *I'm fourteen years old.*	**2** J'ai	et	ans.
3 *I live in Paris.*	**3** J'habite	m'appelle	Paris.
4 *I have a brother and a sister.*	**4** J'ai un frère	joue	une sœur.
5 *I play football.*	**5** Je	quatorze	au foot.

2 🖊 **Write what you think of these things.** (◄◄ pp. 8–9) **Start your sentences with:**

▶ **J'aime** (= I like)   **Je n'aime pas** (= I don't like)
J'adore (= I love)   **Je déteste** (= I hate)

Example: ***J'adore la campagne.***

1 la campagne 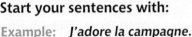 *the country*

2 les magasins *shops*

3 les châteaux *castles*

4 les grandes villes *big towns*

5 les plages *beaches*

6 les villes historiques  *historic towns*

3 📖 **The *same* French word is missing in all three sentences.** (◄◄ pp. 10–11)
Check in the *Sommaire* on page 13.

● What's the missing French word?
● Write the three sentences in English.

1	Je n'ai pas	frère.
2	Je fais	la natation.
3	Il y a beaucoup	collines.

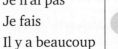

1 a **Write the complete dialogue in your exercise book.**
(◄◄ pp. 6–7)

Example: – *Comment t'appelles-tu?*

– Comment t'appelles-tu?

– Je m'appelle Jérémy.

– Tu as quel âge?

– J'ai quinze ans.

– Tu habites où?

– J'habite à Marseille.

– Tu as des frères et sœurs?

– J'ai un frère. Je n'ai pas de sœur.

– Tu as un passe-temps, Jérémy?

– Oui. Je fais de la natation et je joue au ping-pong.

1 b  extra! **Now write the dialogue with Pauline's answers.**

Profil
- nom: *Pauline Plazenet*
- âge: *14*
- ville: *Versailles*
- frère / sœur: *2 sœurs, 0 frère*
- passe-temps: *vélo, shopping*

Jérémy

Pauline

2 📖 **Read Lise's letter. Then answer the questions in English.**   (◄◄ pp. 8–9)

1 Where in France is Toulouse?

2 Give three reasons why Lise likes the town.

3 Give two reasons why Lise's sister prefers the country.

4 What doesn't Lise like about the country?

5 What two questions does Lise ask Emily at the end of the letter?

> Toulouse, le 20 septembre
>
> Chère Emily,
>
> Je suis ta partenaire française. J'habite à Toulouse, dans le sud-ouest de la France.
>
> J'aime Toulouse: j'aime les distractions et le brouhaha de la ville. J'aime aussi les magasins.
>
> J'ai une sœur. Elle préfère la campagne: elle adore la nature et les animaux. Moi, je n'aime pas l'odeur de fumier!
>
> Et toi, tu préfères la ville ou la campagne? Et tu as un passe-temps?
>
> À bientôt!
>
> Lise

3 a 📖 **Read the sentences with the options given in brackets. One option doesn't make sense! Note the two correct options.**   (◄◄ pp. 10–11)

Example: **1** *centre, nord*

1 J'habite dans le (**centre / plage / nord**) de l'Angleterre.

2 Dans la région il y a beaucoup de (**collines / régions / plages**).

3 Mais il n'y a pas beaucoup de (**vélos / châteaux / villes historiques**).

4 (**J'aime / J'adore / Je joue**) la campagne.

5 J'aime (**les animaux / la pollution / la nature**) à la campagne.

6 Mais j'aime aussi (**les distractions / les frères / les magasins**) en ville.

3 b extra! **Write sentences with two correct and one wrong option, for your partner to solve.**

1 🖎 **Read the English sentences. Then copy out the French sentences correctly. Check your spelling in the *Sommaire* on page 21.**   (◄◄ pp. 14–15)

Example: **1** *J'aime les jeux.*

1 I like TV quiz shows.

2 I don't like comedies.

3 I love soaps.

4 I like cookery programmes.

5 I love sports programmes.

1 J'aime les j _ u _ .

2 Je n'aime pas les c _ m _ d _ e _ .

3 J'adore les s _ r _ es.

4 J'aime les é _ iss _ _ n _ de c _ isi _ e.

5 J'adore les é _ i _ s _ _ n _ de _ po _ _ .

2 📖 **Which French spiral matches which sentence (1–5)?**   (◄◄ pp. 16–17)

Example: **1 E**

1 There's a lot of bad language on TV.
2 There are too many adverts.
3 There isn't too much violence.
4 I don't like talk shows.
5 Too many game shows?
You're joking!

A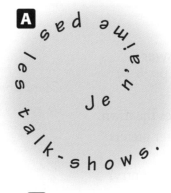
Je n'aime pas les talk-shows.

B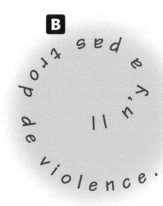
Il n'y a pas trop de violence.

C
Trop de jeux? Tu rigoles!

D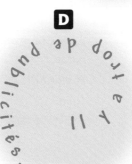
Il y a trop de publicités.

E
Il y a beaucoup de gros mots à la télé.

3 🖎 **These numbers are all written backwards. Write out the French numbers and the figures.**

Example: **1** *dix* – 10

▶

a dix

b quinze

c treize

d cinquante

e trente

f cinq

g seize

h vingt

1 ✎ **Write the opinion for each picture (1–5).** (◀◀ pp. 14–15)

Example: **1** *J'aime les talk-shows.*

> ✓ = j'aime...
> ✗ = je n'aime pas...

les émissions de... cuisine / musique / sport   les jeux   les talk-shows

2 a 📖 **Copy out the discussion filling in the blanks with the right words from the box.** (◀◀ pp. 14–17)

> beaucoup   émissions   les
> violence   préfère   rigoles

2 b ✎ extra! **Write four sentences in French giving your own opinions about TV.**

Example: **1** *Je n'aime pas les émissions de cuisine.*
2 *À mon avis, il n'y a pas trop de violence à la télé.*

▶

Camille	Tu aimes ___¹ séries, toi?
Maxime	Parfois. Mais, il y a trop de ___². Et toi?
Camille	Moi, j'aime les séries. Et j'aime les ___³ de télé-réalité.
Maxime	La télé-réalité?! Tu ___⁴!
Camille	Pourquoi?
Maxime	Les émissions de télé-réalité sont barbantes! Et il y a ___⁵ de gros mots. Moi, je ___⁶ les jeux.

3 a 📖 **Match the clocks with the right times.** (◀◀ pp. 18–19)

Example: **1** C

A Il est quinze heures quarante-cinq.

B Il est vingt heures dix.

C Il est seize heures vingt.

D Il est quinze heures cinq.

E Il est dix-sept heures vingt-cinq.

F Il est dix-huit heures cinquante.

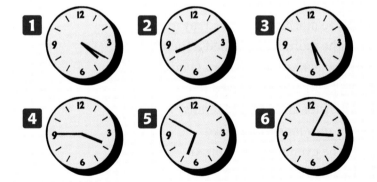

3 b ✎ extra! **Write the times for these clocks. (They are all after midday.)**

1 📖 **Choose one label from the box for each picture.** (◄◄ pp. 24–25)

Example: **1** *le roller coaster*

la grande roue   la barbe à papa
un hot-dog   un jus d'orange
le roller coaster

2 🖊 **Write the numbers in order, from the smallest to the biggest.** (◄◄ pp. 26–27)

Example: *quatre, ...*

cinquante   quatorze   **seize**   **soixante**

six   **quinze**   **quarante**   **quatre**   cinq

3 📖 **Read the French sentences. Which English sentence is the correct translation: a or b?** (◄◄ pp. 28–29)

Example: **1 b**

1 *Le matin, j'ai téléphoné à un copain.*
  a In the morning, I phoned my mum.
  b In the morning, I phoned a friend.

2 *Ma sœur et moi, on a joué au tennis.*
  a My brother and I played tennis.
  b My sister and I played tennis.

3 *Le soir, on a mangé une pizza.*
  a In the evening, I ate a pizza.
  b In the evening, we ate a pizza.

4 *Après ça, on a regardé un film.*
  a After that, we watched a film.
  b After that, we hired a film.

5 *C'était barbant!*
  a It was great!
  b It was boring!

4 📖 **Read the postcard. Answer the questions, and write the *French* word(s) that helped you.** (◄◄ p. 30)

Example: **1 Monday (*lundi*)**

1 Was the trip on Monday or Tuesday?
2 Did they go by car or by coach?
   (**Tip!** Check on page 30.)
3 Did they eat on the beach or in a park?
4 Did they play volleyball or table tennis?
5 Did Nina lose her purse or her camera?

Chère Tante Élise,

Lundi, on a fait une excursion en car. On a visité Strasbourg: c'est une grande ville. Le matin, on a visité le centre.

À midi, on a fait un pique-nique dans un parc.

Après ça, on a joué au volley dans le parc. Mais j'ai perdu mon porte-monnaie!

Nina

1 a ✏️ Unscramble the dialogue, and write it with the words in the correct order. (◀◀ pp. 24–25)

Example: A *Tu as fait un tour sur le roller coaster?*

A [sur] [Tu as] [roller coaster?] [un tour] [fait] [le]

B [j'ai] [Non,] [sur] [fait] [karts.] [un tour] [les]

A [bien?] [C'était]

B [assez] [c'était] [bien.] [Oui,]

A [jus] [acheté] [un] [Tu as] [d'orange?]

B [hot-dog] [acheté] [un] [j'ai] [Non,]

1 b ✏️ extra! Write your own version of the dialogue. Change at least one word in each line.

2 ✏️ Copy out the dialogue, adding in the missing words from the box. (Watch out: there are two extra words!) (◀◀ pp. 26–27)

| Au | C'est | combien | euros |
| la | Voilà | Pardon | pas | Alors |

▶

___, monsieur. C'est ___, cette bague ?

C'est sept ___ cinquante. ___ tout ?

Oui, c'est tout.

___, sept euros cinquante, s'il vous plaît.

___, monsieur.

Merci. ___ revoir.

3 a ✏️ Some letters are missing from these verbs. Write them out correctly. (◀◀ pp. 28–29)

Example: 1 *J'ai téléphoné…*

Don't forget the accents!

1 J'ai t●l●phon● à une copine.

2 On a r●ga●d● des photos.

3 On a jou● au basket.

4 J'ai m●ng● un hot-dog.

5 J'ai t●hat●h● sur Internet.

3 b 📖 Now find the right picture for each sentence.

Example: 1 **C**

 A
 **B**
 **C**
 **D**
 **E**

4 📖 extra! Match up the half-sentences to produce a description of an outing. (◀◀ p. 30)

1 Mercredi, on a fait…   … dans un restaurant.

2 À midi, on a visité…   … super-génial!

3 Mais après ça, j'ai perdu…   … mon appareil-photo.

4 Le soir, on a mangé…   … un grand château.

5 C'était…   … une excursion en famille.

1 📖 **Write out the sentences properly and find the English to match.**   (◄◄ pp. 32–33)

Example: **1** *J'aime Alizée. – I like Alizée.*

1 J'aimeAlizée.

2 J'aimesamusique.

3 Elleabeaucoupdetalent.

4 J'aimesesvêtements.

5 J'aimesonlook.

I like her clothes.
I like Alizée.
I like her image.
She's very talented.
I like her music.

2 a ✏️ **Follow the lines and write out the full sentences.**   (◄◄ pp. 34–35)

Example: **1** *J'aime Avril Lavigne parce que j'aime sa musique.*

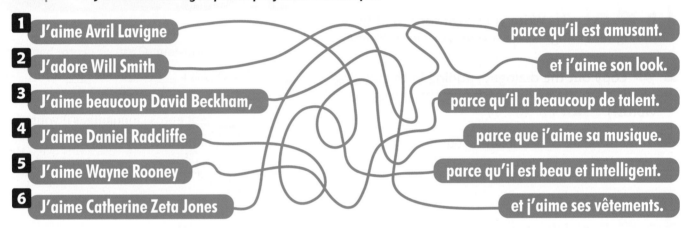

1 J'aime Avril Lavigne

2 J'adore Will Smith

3 J'aime beaucoup David Beckham,

4 J'aime Daniel Radcliffe

5 J'aime Wayne Rooney

6 J'aime Catherine Zeta Jones

parce qu'il est amusant.

et j'aime son look.

parce qu'il a beaucoup de talent.

parce que j'aime sa musique.

parce qu'il est beau et intelligent.

et j'aime ses vêtements.

2 b 📖 **Add a tick if you agree with a sentence, and a cross if you don't agree.**

3 ✏️ **Write a correct sentence for each picture (1–5).**   (◄◄ pp. 36–37)

Example: **1** *Éric ne boit pas beaucoup d'alcool.*

1 Éric (**boit**) / (**ne boit**) pas beaucoup d'alcool.

2 Il (**fume**) / (**ne fume**) pas.

3 Il (**mange**) / (**ne mange pas**) beaucoup de fruits et de légumes.

4 Il (**se drogue**) / (**ne se drogue pas**).

5 Il (**fait**) / (**ne fait pas**) beaucoup d'exercice.

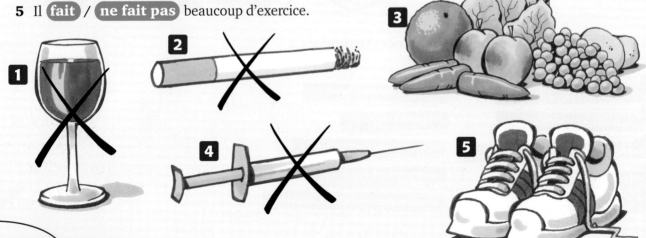

1 ✏️ **Copy these sentences adding in names of your choice!** (◄◄ pp. 32–33)

Example: **1** *J'aime Dr Dre: j'adore sa musique.*

1 J'aime __: j'adore sa musique.

2 J'adore __. Il a beaucoup de talent.

3 Moi, j'aime __. J'aime ses vêtements.

4 Tu aimes __? Moi, j'adore son look.

5 J'aime __. Elle a beaucoup de talent.

Remember:
- *son*, *sa* and *ses* can mean 'his' **or** 'her', so you can choose a man or a woman
- *il* = he; *elle* = she

2 📖 **Are these sentences logical** 😃 **or silly** 😜 (◄◄ pp. 34–35)
extra! **Change the silly sentences so that they make sense.**

Example: **1** 😜 (*extra!* *J'aime Avril Lavigne parce que j'aime sa musique.*)

1 Je n'aime pas Avril Lavigne parce que j'aime sa musique.

2 J'aime beaucoup David Beckham, et j'aime ses vêtements.

3 Je n'aime pas Daniel Radcliffe parce qu'il est beau et intelligent.

4 J'adore Will Smith parce qu'il n'est pas amusant.

5 J'aime Wayne Rooney parce qu'il a beaucoup de talent.

6 J'aime Catherine Zeta Jones parce que je n'aime pas son look.

3 a ✏️ **Unjumble the captions for these pictures.**
(◄◄ pp. 36–37)

Example: **1** *Anne ne boit pas beaucoup d'alcool.*

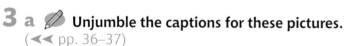

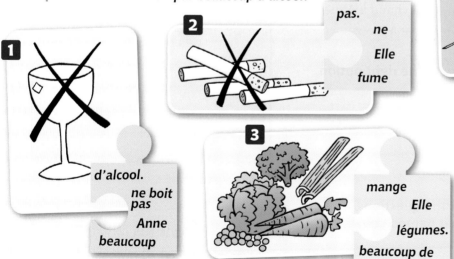

1 d'alcool. ne boit pas Anne beaucoup

2 pas. ne Elle fume

3 mange Elle légumes. beaucoup de

4 ne pas. se drogue Elle

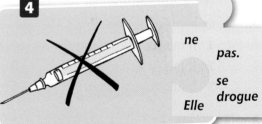

5 beaucoup fait Elle d'exercice.

6 ne mange pas beaucoup Elle de fruits.

3 b ✏️ *extra!* **Make these sentences negative, using *ne ... pas*.**

Example: **1** *Sophie **ne** regarde **pas** la télé.*

1 Sophie regarde la télé.

2 Elle mange à la cantine.

3 Elle fait beaucoup de sport.

4 Elle joue au tennis de table.

5 Elle boit beaucoup de jus d'orange.

6 Elle travaille à Paris.

1 ✏️ **Write the name of the shop where you could buy items 1–6.** (◄◄ pp. 42–43)

Example: **1** *la charcuterie*

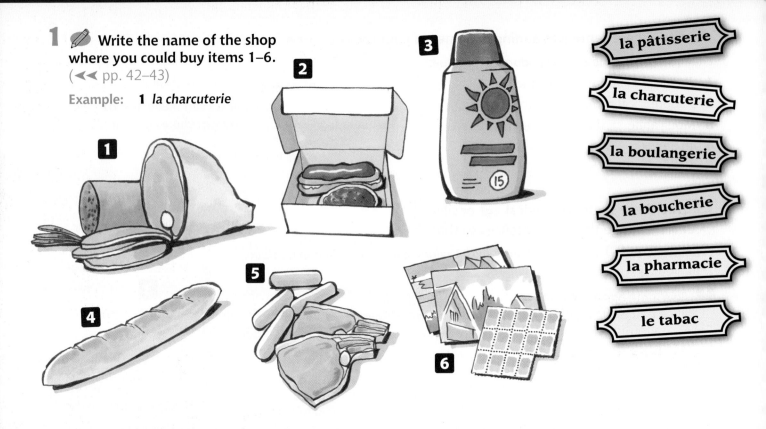

la pâtisserie

la charcuterie

la boulangerie

la boucherie

la pharmacie

le tabac

2 a 📖 **Look at the map. True or false (1–6)?** (◄◄ pp. 46–47)

Example: **1** true

1 Il fait mauvais à Nantes.
2 Il fait froid à Marseille.
3 Il fait beau à Lyon.
4 Il neige à Lille.
5 Il fait chaud à Annecy.
6 Il pleut à Metz.

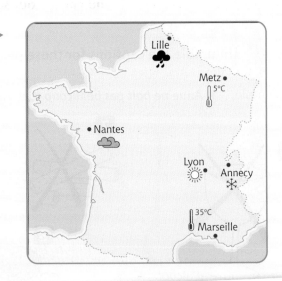

2 b ✏️ **Copy out the sentences with the right option.**

1 Lille est dans le nord / le sud.
2 Nantes est dans l'est / l'ouest.
3 Marseille est dans le nord / le sud.
4 Annecy est dans l'est / l'ouest.

3 📖 **Read the postcard. Answer the questions, and write the *French* word(s) that helped you.** (◄◄ p.48)

Example: **1** south (*sud*)

1 Is Sète in the south or the north of France?
2 Is the weather hot or cold?
3 Does Marc like or dislike the weather?
4 Can you go to the hills or to the beach?
5 Does Marc like or dislike going on trips?

Salut!

Je suis à Sète, dans le sud de la France. Il fait très, très chaud. J'aime ça!

On peut aller à la plage. Et on peut faire du karting. J'adore ça!

On peut aussi faire des excursions, mais je n'aime pas les excursions!

Marc

1 ✏️ **Copy the dialogue, separating the words as necessary.**
(◀◀ pp. 42–43)

Example: – *Pardon, madame. Il y...*

> pardonmada
> meilyaunepâti
> sserieprèsd'iciou
> idanslarueDiderotc
> 'estloinnonc'estàcinqm
> inutesmercimadameaurevoir

2 a ✏️ **Write out the dialogue with the words in the correct order.**
(◀◀ pp. 44–45)

– monsieur. | Bonjour | vous aider? | peux | Je
– Oui. | du karting | à Biarritz? | peut | On | faire
– bien | Oui, | sûr.
– brochure? | Avez-vous | une
– monsieur. | Oui, | Voilà.

2 b ✏️ **Write four more questions you could ask in the second line of the dialogue. Then look back at the *Sommaire* on page 49 and check your spelling.**

3 📖 **Complete the email with words from the box.** (◀◀ pp. 46–47)

Example: **1** *m'appelle*

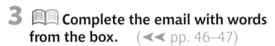

beaucoup   C'est   dans   fait
les   m'appelle   On   peut

> Salut. Je ___¹ Julien.
> J'habite à La Rochelle, ___² l'ouest de la France.
> ___³ une belle ville historique. En été, il ___⁴ beau et il y a ___⁵ de touristes. Ils aiment ___⁶ belles plages.
> À La Rochelle, on ___⁷ faire du surf. ___⁸ peut aussi faire des excursions. La Rochelle, c'est super!

4 a 📖 **Read the text. True or false?**
(◀◀ p. 48)

1 It's very hot in Cabourg.
2 Mélanie likes Cabourg.
3 You can go horse-riding.
4 You can't hire bikes.
5 There's a good cake shop nearby.

4 b ✏️ extra! **Copy the postcard, but change one part of each sentence.**

Example: **Bonjour! Je suis à Biarritz. Il...**

> Salut!
> Je suis à Cabourg. Il fait mauvais: il fait vraiment froid! Mais c'est fantastique ici.
> À Cabourg, on peut aller à la plage et on peut faire du cheval. On peut aussi louer des vélos. Mais on ne peut pas faire du surf: il fait trop froid! Il y a une pâtisserie excellente près de l'hôtel!
> À bientôt!
> Mélanie

1 ✏️ **Write a sentence for each picture.** (◀◀ pp. 50–51)

Example: **1** *J'ai mal au dos.*

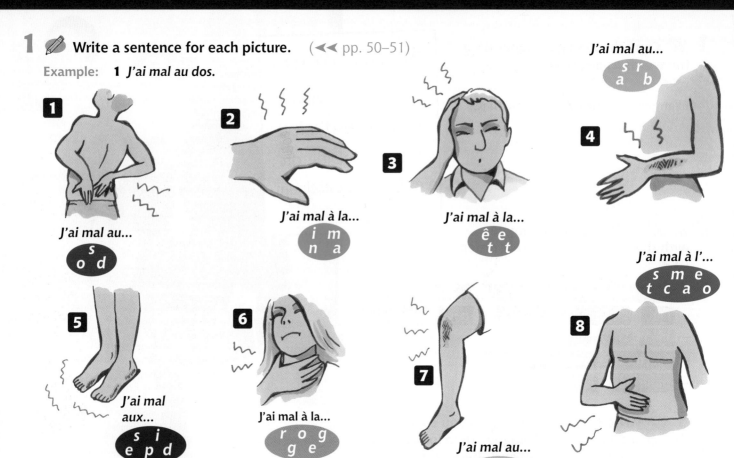

J'ai mal au...
s o d

J'ai mal à la...
i m n a

J'ai mal à la...
ê e t t

J'ai mal au...
s r a b

J'ai mal à l'...
s m e t c a o

J'ai mal aux...
s i e p d

J'ai mal à la...
r o g g e

J'ai mal au...
u o g n e

2 📖 **Read the English sentences. Write the French sentence with the correct option.** (◀◀ pp. 52–53)

Example: **1** *Lundi dernier, M. Blanc a téléphoné à son bureau.*

Last Monday, Mr Blanc phoned his office.   **1** Lundi / Mardi dernier, M. Blanc a téléphoné à son bureau.

'I've got a headache.'   **2** "J'ai mal au dos / à la tête."

Mr Blanc went to the stadium.   **3** M. Blanc est allé / arrivé au stade.

He watched the tennis.   **4** Il a écouté / regardé le tennis.

'Look at this photo!'   **5** "Mangez / Regardez cette photo!"

3 📖 **Find the missing words in the box and write out the complete dialogue.** (◀◀ pp. 54–55)

Depuis mal ou pas une va

– Salut, Vincent. Ça ___ ?
– Non. J'ai ___ à la gorge.
– Oh là là! ___ longtemps?
– Depuis quatre ___ cinq jours... Non, depuis ___ semaine.
– Hmm... Ce n'est ___ amusant, ça!

1 ✏ **Write a sentence for each person in the doctor's waiting room.**   (◂◂ pp. 50–51)

extra! **Write the sentences from memory, then check your spelling.**

Example: **1** *J'ai mal à la main.*

2 📖 **Unjumble the story and write the letters (A–I) in the correct order.**   (◂◂ pp. 52–53)

Example: **C, G, ✦, ✦ , ✦, A,✦, B,✦**

A Lundi, M. Blanc est allé au bureau.

B Le patron: "Regardez cette photo!"

C M. Blanc habite à Paris. Il adore le tennis.

D Le patron: "OK! Pas de problème!"

E Mal au dos? Mal à la tête? Non! M. Blanc est allé regarder le tennis!

F Le patron: "Vous êtes allé regarder le tennis! Vous êtes renvoyé!"

G La semaine dernière, il a téléphoné à son bureau.

H M. Blanc: "Je ne peux pas venir travailler. J'ai mal au dos. J'ai mal à la tête!"

I M. Blanc: "La semaine dernière, c'était horrible!"

3 a ✏ **Can you write the six missing words? Look back at page 54 if you get stuck.**   (◂◂ pp. 54–55)

3 b ✏ extra! **Write your own version of the dialogue: change the words in red.**

Example: *va, ...*

– Bonjour, Antoine. Ça (★) ?

– Non... J'ai (★) à l'estomac.

– Ah oui? (★) longtemps?

– Depuis trois jours.

– Hmm... Ce n'est (★) amusant, ça!

– Maman, je (★) jouer dans le match de foot samedi?

– Oui, (★) sûr.

1 a ✏️ Copy and complete the eight labels. (◀◀ pp. 58–59)

Example: **1** *les gâteaux au chocolat*

1 les gâ★eau★ au cho★ola★

2 les c★rot★es

3 la v★and★

4 le ju★ d'or★n★e

5 l'★a★

6 les p★mm★s de te★★e

7 la ★ou★e

8 les pâ★e★

1 b ✏️ Write two sentences with *j'aime* (I like) to say which foods and drinks you like.

Example: *J'aime la soupe. – I like soup.*

2 📖 Read the text below, then say whether 1–6 are true or false. (◀◀ pp. 58–61)

Example: **1 true**

1 Arthur is hungry.
2 He's also very thirsty.
3 Coralie is offered carrots.
4 She prefers chips.
5 Arthur asks for the ham.
6 He is given bread and ham.

Bon appétit! Tu as faim, Arthur?

Tu as soif?

Oui.

Non, pas beaucoup.

Tu aimes les pâtes, Coralie?

Non. Je préfère les frites.

Je peux avoir le jambon, s'il vous plaît?

Oui, voilà le pain et le jambon.

1 ✎ **Write the dialogue with the words in correct order.** (◄◄ pp. 58–59)

- appétit! Bon
- faim, as Victor? Tu
- j'ai Oui, faim
- aimes Tu viande? la
- beaucoup Oui,
- Victor? aimes jus d'orange le Tu
- Non, beaucoup pas. l'eau préfère Je

2 ✎ **Copy CHOCOLAT, written vertically, down the middle of your page. Then write food words to connect horizontally.** (◄◄ pp. 58–61)

Can you find one for each letter?

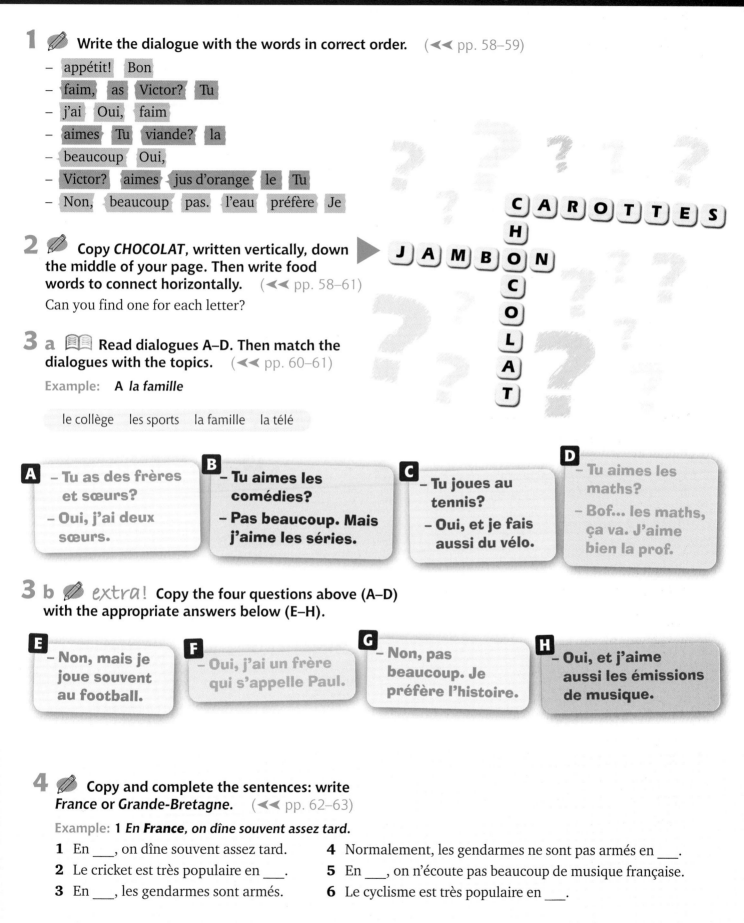

3 a 📖 **Read dialogues A–D. Then match the dialogues with the topics.** (◄◄ pp. 60–61)

Example: **A** *la famille*

le collège   les sports   la famille   la télé

A
– Tu as des frères et sœurs?
– Oui, j'ai deux sœurs.

B
– Tu aimes les comédies?
– Pas beaucoup. Mais j'aime les séries.

C
– Tu joues au tennis?
– Oui, et je fais aussi du vélo.

D
– Tu aimes les maths?
– Bof... les maths, ça va. J'aime bien la prof.

3 b ✎ *extra!* **Copy the four questions above (A–D) with the appropriate answers below (E–H).**

E
– Non, mais je joue souvent au football.

F
– Oui, j'ai un frère qui s'appelle Paul.

G
– Non, pas beaucoup. Je préfère l'histoire.

H
– Oui, et j'aime aussi les émissions de musique.

4 ✎ **Copy and complete the sentences: write France or Grande-Bretagne.** (◄◄ pp. 62–63)

Example: 1 *En France, on dîne souvent assez tard.*

1 En ___, on dîne souvent assez tard.

2 Le cricket est très populaire en ___.

3 En ___, les gendarmes sont armés.

4 Normalement, les gendarmes ne sont pas armés en ___.

5 En ___, on n'écoute pas beaucoup de musique française.

6 Le cyclisme est très populaire en ___.

1 📖 **Read the four newspaper headlines (A–D).** (◄◄ pp. 64–65)

Copy the newspaper headline which has a story about:

1 a divorce
2 a wedding
3 someone going out with an actress
4 the birth of a baby

A

Diane a épousé Romain!

B

Carla Carlier a eu un bébé!

C

Jérémy Mordin a divorcé de Yasmine!

D

Nathan Bourdas sort avec l'actrice Juliette Delémont

2 ✏️ **Look at the puzzle. Then copy and complete 1–6 below.**

Use the letters in the puzzle to help you. (◄◄ pp. 66–67)

Example: 1 des **a**gend**a**s

1 des ✱gend✱s
2 de✱ CD vierge✱
3 de✱ jour✱aux a✱glais
4 ✱es ✱V✱
5 d✱s rang✱-CD
6 des écout✱rs

3 📖 **Read the French dialogue, then copy and complete the English dialogue.** (◄◄ pp. 66–67)

Example:
Excuse me. Do you have... ?

Pardon, madame. Avez-vous des écouteurs? — *Excuse me. Do you ___ headphones?*

Oui, en haut. — *Yes, ___.*

Pardon, pouvez-vous répéter? — *Sorry, could you ___?*

Ils sont en haut. — *They ___ upstairs.*

Ah! Merci beaucoup. — *Ah! ___ a lot.*

De rien. — *Don't mention it.*

4 ✏️ **Read the French report and note the correct words in the English version.** (◄◄ p. 68)

Lundi soir, un incendie a ravagé une pâtisserie.
Les pompiers sont arrivés immédiatement.
Une ambulance est arrivée dix minutes plus tard.
La police a arrêté deux suspects.

On **1** *Monday / Tuesday evening, a fire damaged a* **2** *supermarket / cake shop. The fire brigade arrived* **3** *quickly / immediately. An ambulance arrived* **4** *five / ten minutes later. The police arrested* **5** *two / three suspects.*

1 📖 **Read the biography, then answer the questions in English.** (◀◀ pp. 64–65)

1 When did Lola arrive in France?
2 Who did she marry?
3 What was her husband's work?
4 What happened when she was 20?
5 Where did she go after the divorce?
6 What does her new boyfriend do?

Lola Luline

Lola Luline est une chanteuse célèbre. Elle est arrivée en France en 1999.

Lola a épousé Richard Grandet, le pianiste, et elle a eu son premier bébé à l'âge de 20 ans.

Mais il y a eu des problèmes, et Lola a divorcé de Richard. Elle est allée en Italie.

Maintenant, Lola habite à Rome. Elle sort avec l'acteur Paulo Prodi.

2 ✏️ **Write a question for each picture (A–F).** (◀◀ pp. 66–67)

Example: A *Avez-vous des DVD?*

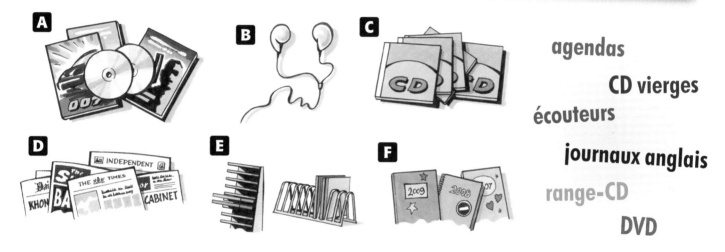

agendas

CD vierges

écouteurs

journaux anglais

range-CD

DVD

3 ✏️ **Look again at the dialogue on page 67. Then copy the sentences, filling in the missing vowels.**

Example: **1** *Avez-vous des CD vierges?*

1 **vz-vs ds CD vrgs?**
2 **ls snt n ht**
3 **Prdn, pvz-vs rptr?**
4 **Mrc, mnsr**
5 **D rn**

4 ✏️ **Copy the newspaper report, filling in the gaps with the words in the box.** (◀◀ p. 68)

pharmacie   immediatement
minutes   quatre   jeudi

___¹ soir, un incendie a ravagé une ___². Les pompiers sont arrivés ___³. Une ambulance est arrivée quinze ___⁴ plus tard. La police a arrêté ___⁵ suspects.

1 ✏️ **Look at sentences 1–5 in English. Then write sentences 1–5 in French, choosing the right words from the middle column.** (◄◄ pp. 72–73)

Example: **1 J'aime beaucoup faire du sport.**

1	I	really like	doing sport	**1**	J'	déteste	faire du sport.
2	I	love	dancing.	**2**	J'	aime beaucoup	danser.
3	I	hate	cooking.	**3**	Je	préfère	faire la cuisine.
4	I	don't like	playing cards.	**4**	Je	adore	jouer aux cartes.
5	I	prefer	going round the shops.	**5**	Je	n'aime pas	faire les magasins.

2 ✏️ **Look at the words in the boxes, then write these two sentences in French.** (◄◄ pp. 74–75)

Example: **Théo est heureux, ...**

1 Théo is happy, sporty, shy and musical.

2 Stéphanie is funny, extrovert, cheeky and lazy.

Théo est   heur-   -cien
spor-   -mide
ti-   -tif
musi-   -eux

Stéphanie est   amu-   -seuse
extra-   -sante
imper-   -vertie
pares-   -tinente

3 📖 **Read the text and answer the questions in English.** (◄◄ p. 76)

1 When did Christophe go into the house?

2 How many other people were there?

3 Which person was very musical?

4 When did they have a barbecue?

5 In which week did Christophe have to leave the house?

> *La Maison Verte*
>
> *J'adore la télé-réalité! Le 30 mai, je suis entré dans la Maison Verte. C'était vraiment génial!*
>
> *Il y avait huit autres personnes. Simon était très musicien. Claudia était vraiment amusante!*
>
> *Le dimanche, on a fait un barbecue.*
>
> *Mais désastre! La première semaine, j'ai dû quitter la Maison!*
>
> *Christophe*

1 ✏️ **Write a sentence for each picture (A–H).**

If you get stuck, look at the *Sommaire* on page 77.
(◄◄ pp. 72–73)

✔ = *J'aime beaucoup…*

✗ = *Je n'aime pas…*

Example: **A** *Je n'aime pas danser.*

2 a 📖 **Read the texts. Who is… ?**

(◄◄ pp. 74–75)

1 quite musical
2 very sporty
3 really funny
4 often lazy
5 sometimes cheeky

Je suis extraverti et parfois impertinent. À mon avis, je suis vraiment amusant!

Émilien

Alice

Je suis assez musicienne et très sportive, mais je suis souvent paresseuse.

2 b ✏️ extra! **Write the sentences out correctly. Then write what they mean in English.**

Example: *Je suis très heureuse.* – I am very happy.

1 suis Je heureuse. très
2 Je ne jamais paresseux. suis
3 timide. Je toujours vraiment suis
4 assez Ma sœur impertinente. est parfois
5 très est vraiment musicien. Mon frère
6 ne sportif. Je très suis pas

3 ✏️ **Match the sentence beginnings and endings to write sentences about the TV show *La Maison Bleue*.** (◄◄ p. 76)

1 En mars, j'ai fait…	la *Maison Bleue*.
2 J'ai envoyé ma vidéo…	à la BBC.
3 Dix semaines plus tard,…	génial!
4 En juillet, je suis entré dans…	la première semaine.
5 C'était vraiment…	je suis allé à Manchester pour une audition.
6 Mais j'ai dû quitter la maison…	une vidéo.

1 📖 **Match the questions and answers.** (◄◄ pp. 78–79)

Example: **1 c**

1 C'est quoi, ton adresse e-mail?

2 Tu aimes quelle sorte de musique?

3 Tu supportes une équipe de football?

4 Tu veux des chips?

5 Comment t'appelles-tu?

a J'aime la musique d'Alizée.

b Je m'appelle Max.

c C'est SRF@libertysurf.fr

d Oui, je supporte Lille O.S.C.

e Non, merci.

2 ✏️ **Write the correct sentence for each picture.** (◄◄ pp. 80–81)

Example: **1** *On est allé à la mer.*

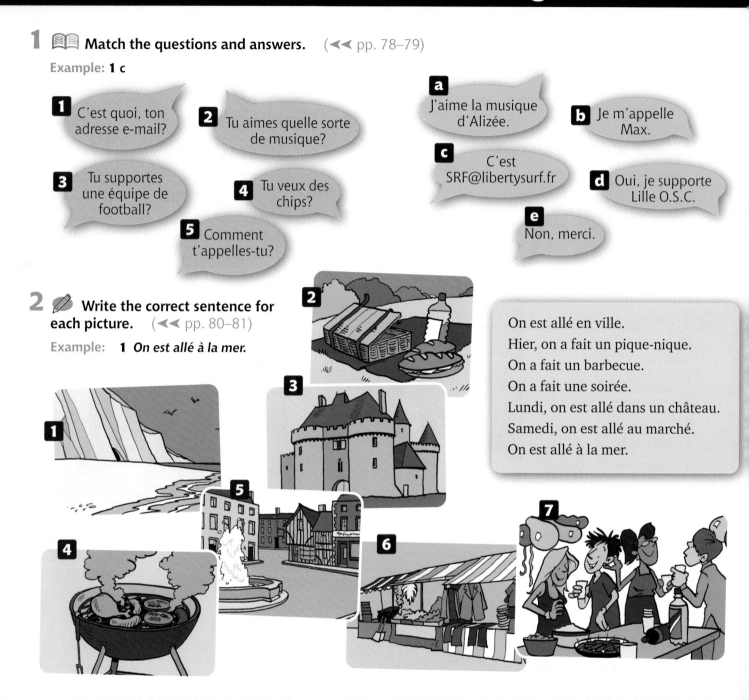

On est allé en ville.
Hier, on a fait un pique-nique.
On a fait un barbecue.
On a fait une soirée.
Lundi, on est allé dans un château.
Samedi, on est allé au marché.
On est allé à la mer.

3 ✏️ **Read the English sentences, then write the French sentences correctly.**

Check the *Sommaire* on page 83 if you need to. (◄◄ pp. 82–83)

Example: **1** *Allô, c'est Kévin.*

1 *Hello, it's Kévin.*

2 *It was super in York*

3 *I really liked the cricket.*

4 *It was brilliant.*

5 *Thanks for everything.*

6 *Say hello to your family.*

1 c'est   Kévin.   Allô,

2 à York   super   C'était

3 le   J'ai   cricket.   beaucoup aimé

4 top.   le   C'était

5 pour   Merci   tout.

6 famille.   Bonjour à   ta

1 a 📖 Read the dialogue and find the missing words. (◀◀ pp. 78–79)

adresse   C'est   comment   équipe   m'appelle   musique   pas   quelle

Example: 1 comment

– Salut, ___¹ t'appelles-tu?

– Je ___² Aurélia.

– Tu aimes ___³ sorte de musique?

– J'aime la ___⁴ de *Crismatic*.

– C'est quoi, ton ___⁵ e-mail?

– ___⁶ ATP@yahoo.fr

– Tu supportes une ___⁷ de football?

– Non, je n'aime ___⁸ le football.

1 b ✏️ extra! Write a gapped dialogue for your partner to fill in.

2 ✏️ Anagrams! Write the captions out correctly. (◀◀ pp. 80–81)

Example: 1 Lundi, on est allé dans un...

1 NULDI, on est allé dans un EAUTÂCH. C'était UMASANT.

2 Mardi, on a fait une OIRSÉE. C'était INÉGAL.

3 HIRE, on est allé au CHÉRAM. C'était BINE.

4 Le soir, on a FATI un RABCEBUE. C'était UPSER.

3 📖 Read the thank you letter and answer the questions. (◀◀ pp. 82–83)

1 What two things did Mathilde really like?

2 What did she do yesterday?

3 What did she think of it?

extra!

4 Where is the park she mentions?

5 What is she going to do on Saturday and Sunday?

Chère Camille,

C'était super à Marseille: merci beaucoup pour tout! J'ai beaucoup aimé le château et les jeux à la maison.

Hier, on est allé à un concert dans le parc près du collège. C'était vraiment nul!!

Samedi, on va faire de la natation et dimanche, on va faire du cheval.

À+

Mathilde

1 ✏️ **Check the meanings of the following opinions in the Sommaire on page 91.** (◄◄ pp. 86–87)

Then write the positive opinions in one list and the negative opinions in another.

C'est intéressant.

C'est pénible.

C'est nul.

C'est amusant.

C'est génial.

C'est archinul.

C'est vraiment top.

C'est barbant.

It's interesting.	It's fun.
It's really great.	It's great.
It's a pain.	It's boring.
It's complete rubbish.	It's rubbish.

Example:

opinions positives ✓	opinions négatives ✗
C'est amusant. – *It's fun.*	

2 📖 **One letter is missing in each line. Which letter is it?** (◄◄ pp. 86–87)

Example:　**1 the letter O**

1 J'aime la b✶xe et la C✶upe du m✶nde.
2 Tu ✶imes le g✶ngster✶p? – Oui, c'est ✶mus✶nt!
3 Je d✶teste la t✶l✶-r✶alit✶. C'est p✶nible!
4 La ✶oxe, c'est ✶ar✶ant!
5 J'a✶me la pol✶t✶que. C'est ✶ntéressant.
6 Q✶oi? T✶rigoles? C'est archin✶l!

3 📖 **Read the English discussion on zoos. Then write the French dialogue, putting the sentences in the right order.** (◄◄ pp. 88–89)

Hugo	*Are you for or against zoos?*
Éva	*I'm against.*
Hugo	*Why?*
Éva	*The cages are too small. It's cruel!*
Hugo	*But going to the zoo is fun.*
Éva	*It's no fun for the animals!*

– Pourquoi?

– Mais aller au zoo, c'est amusant.

– Moi, je suis contre.

– Les cages sont trop petites. C'est cruel!

– Ce n'est pas amusant pour les animaux!

– Tu es pour ou contre les zoos?

4 📖 **Quiz! True or false?**

1 There are more tigers in captivity than in the wild.
2 Black rhinos are more common than white rhinos.
3 There are more elephants in Africa than in Asia.
4 Penguins and polar bears often live near each other.
● Now check your answers on page 90!

1 **In sentences 1–5, each symbol represents two letters. Can you crack the code?**
(◄◄ pp. 86–87)

● Write the sentences in correct French.

● Say what these symbols represent:

| ♦ | ♥ | ♠ | ♣ |

Example:

1 *La télé-réalité, c'est pénible.* (Symbol ♦ = es)

> **1** La télé-réalité, c'♦t pénible.
> **2** J'ado♥ la boxe. C'♦t vraiment top!
> **3** Moi, j'ado♥ la politique: c'♦t très inté♥ss♠t.
> **4** Et moi, je dét♦te la politique. C'♦t barb♠t!
> **5** Quoi? Tu rigol♦? C'♦t très amus♠t!
> **6** Tu aim♦ la C♣pe du monde?

2 **Write what *you* think of each activity (A–F).**
(◄◄ pp. 86–87)

Example: **A** *J'adore la télé-réalité. C'est amusant.*

| j'aime | | j'adore | | je n'aime pas | | je déteste |

3 a  **Be careful: there's a word missing in each sentence! Write the complete sentences with the missing word from the box.**   (◄◄ pp. 88–89)

| au | es | les |
| pas | ce | sont |

Example: **1** *Tu **es** pour ou contre les zoos?*

1 Tu pour ou contre les zoos?

2 Aller zoo, c'est intéressant.

3 Ce n'est amusant pour les animaux.

4 Les cages trop petites.

5 Les zoos préservent animaux en danger.

6 Mais non, n'est pas vrai!

3 b ✎ **extra!** **Invent a similar 'missing words puzzle' for your partner.**

1  Copy these headings: **people**   **a time**   **a place**

Then copy the words below under the right heading.

(If you've forgotten the words, you'll find them in the *Glossaire*, (◄◄ pp. 133–141)

Example:

people
deux frères

deux frères   dimanche   une boulangerie   samedi   la piscine   en août
ma star préférée   la gare   trois heures   ma famille   la patinoire   une sœur
le week-end dernier   les copains   le centre sportif   mardi après-midi

2 a 🖊 **Copy the questions, separating out the words.**   (◄◄ pp. 92–93)

Example: **1** *C'est qui, ta star préférée?*

1
c'estqui,
tastar
préférée?

2
tuas
desfrères
etsœurs?

3
tues
pourou
contreleszoos?

4
tuaimes
lesséries
àlatélé?

5
tuas
faitquoile
week-enddernier?

2 b 📖 **Now match each French question in 2a with one of the questions below.**

Example: **1** *C'est qui, ta star préférée?* – b

a Do you like series on TV?
b Who is your favourite star?
c Are you for or against zoos?
d What did you do last weekend?
e Do you have any brothers and sisters?

3 📖 **Read the emails. Who is talking about… ?**

a her family   **b** her favourite star   **c** TV   **d** last weekend   **e** what he thinks about zoos

Moi, à la télé, j'aime les séries
et les émissions de musique.
Léa

Ma star préférée, c'est Avril
Lavigne. Elle est très originale.
Justine

Je suis contre les zoos.
Les cages sont beaucoup
trop petites! C'est cruel!
Hamed

J'ai une sœur, Sarah, et je n'ai
pas de frère. Mon père est prof,
et ma mère est vétérinaire.
Régine

Le week-end dernier, je suis
allé au cinéma. J'ai vu un film
américain avec Mel Gibson.
Sébastien

1 📖 **Read questions 1–7 below. Then read the newspaper article and choose the right options: a or b.**

Example: **1 b**

A 1 The reception was on   **a** Friday evening   **b** Saturday evening.

2 It was for   **a** twenty pupils   **b** fifty pupils.

B 3 Sabine Meyer is   **a** Swiss   **b** German.

4 Next year, Sadiq plans to go to   **a** New York   **b** Barcelona.

C 5 On Sunday morning the pupils   **a** saw the sites in Paris   **b** had a lie-in.

6 They were given lunch on the first floor of   **a** the hotel Louis XIV   **b** the Eiffel Tower.

7 The bus then took the pupils to   **a** the airport   **b** the railway station.

Réception à l'hôtel Louis XIV

A Samedi soir, l'Association Nationale du Français a organisé une réception pour vingt élèves européens à l'hôtel Louis XIV.

B "C'était une réception superbe," a dit Sabine Meyer (14), qui est allemande et habite à Berlin.
"J'ai bavardé avec une fille de Barcelone," a dit Sadiq Akbar, qui habite à York, en Angleterre. "Et l'année prochaine, je vais lui rendre visite à Barcelone."

C Dimanche matin, les élèves ont visité les sites de Paris en bus. Ils ont déjeuné au premier étage de la tour Eiffel, et puis ils sont retournés en bus à l'aéroport Charles de Gaulle.

2 ✏️ **Write six sentences by choosing the right elements from each column.**

Example: **1** *J'ai un frère et une sœur.*

1 J'ai un frère	une excursion	un film.
2 J'aime	les séries	sœur.
3 Samedi dernier, on a	regardé	Robbie Williams.
4 On a fait	et une	les zoos.
5 Ma star préférée,	pour	à Londres.
6 Je suis	c'est	à la télé.

3 📖 **Which is the odd one out, and why?** *extra!* **Write your own puzzle for your partner.**

1
mon frère
ma sœur
mon cousin
mon grand-père

2
les chats
les lions
les zoos
les tigres

3
les séries
les comédies
les stars
les talk-shows

4
amusant
barbant
super
intéressant

5
mercredi
dimanche
le week-end
samedi

Grammaire *Contents*

- Use these pages to check up on any grammar point you're not quite sure of.
- If you're still not clear about any point, ask your teacher.

Here's an example to show where you can find explanations of various parts of a French sentence:

l' A2.1   **tu** C2   **un** A2.2   *adjectives* A3   *nouns* A1

- **L'après-midi, tu as acheté un album de photos noir au magasin?**

après-midi   **as acheté**   *word order* E4   **au**   *questions* E2
(when/how often) F4   *(past tense)* B4.1   *(prepositions)* D1.2

Glossary of terms

- **Adjectives** Les adjectifs
  ... are words that describe somebody or something:
  grand *big*, **vert** *green*

- **Determiners**
  ... come before nouns and limit them:
  les *the*, **un** *a*, **ma** *my*

- **The infinitive** L'infinitif
  ... is the 'name' of the verb, as listed in a dictionary:
  jouer *to play*, **aller** *to go*

- **Nouns** Les substantifs
  ... are words for somebody or something:
  frère *brother*, **musique** *music*

- **Prepositions** Les prépositions
  ... are words used with nouns to give information about when, how, where, etc.
  à *at, in, to*   **pour** *for*
  avec *with*   **dans** *in*

- **Pronouns** Les pronoms
  ... are short words used instead of a noun or name:
  je *I*, **tu** *you*, **il** *he*, **elle** *she*

- **Singular and plural** Singulier et pluriel
  Singular refers to just <u>one</u> thing or person:
  chat *cat*, **sœur** *sister*

  Plural refers to more than one thing or person:
  chats *cats*, **sœurs** *sisters*

- **Verbs** Les verbes
  Verbs express an action or a state:
  j'**habite** *I live*
  j'**ai** *I have*
  elle **aime** *she likes*

A Masculine and feminine, singular and plural

A1 *Les noms* Nouns

A1.1 Singular and plural nouns

- As in English, French nouns can be singular or plural. Most plural nouns end in -s:
  1 frère, 2 frères *1 brother, 2 brothers*

  Unlike in English, the added -s is usually <u>not</u> pronounced.

- Some French nouns take a different ending in the plural:
  1 château, 2 châteaux *1 castle, 2 castles*
  The 'x' is not pronounced.

A1.2 Masculine and feminine nouns

- One key difference between English and French grammar is that <u>all</u> French nouns fall into one of two categories. We call these categories **masculine** and **feminine**.
  For example: **château, film, vélo, musée** are all masculine nouns.
  ville, limonade, danse, plage are all feminine nouns.

- Some nouns have a masculine and a feminine form:
  le prof *the male teacher*   **la prof** *the female teacher*

- Other nouns have two different forms:
  un copain *a male friend*   **une copine** *a female friend*

A2 Determiners

A2.1 le, la, les *the*

- The word for 'the' depends on whether the noun is masculine or feminine, singular or plural.

masculine singular	feminine singular	masculine and feminine plural
le	la	les

le chat *the cat*   la ville *the town*   les magasins *the shops*

If singular nouns begin with a vowel or a silent *h*, **le** and **la** are shortened to **l'**: **l'animal** *the animal*

- **le**, **la** and **les** are sometimes used when we don't say 'the' in English:
  la capitale de **la** France *the capital of France*
  Je rentre à **la** maison. *I go home.*

- **le** is also used with expressions of time:
  le soir *in the evening*
  le matin *in the morning*
  le week-end *at the weekend*
  le lundi *on Mondays*
  le lundi après-midi *on Monday afternoons*
  (**lundi** *on one particular Monday*)

A2.2 un, une *a, an*

- The word for 'a' or 'an' depends on whether the noun is masculine or feminine.

masculine singular	feminine singular
un	une

un village *a village*   une ambulance *an ambulance*

A2.3 du, de la, de l', des *some*

- Like the words for 'the', the words for 'some' depend on whether the noun is masculine or feminine, singular or plural.

	masculine singular*	feminine singular*	masculine and femine plural
some	du	de la	des

*if the singular noun starts with a vowel or silent *h*
de l'

du lait *some milk*   **des** carottes *carrots*
de la salade *some salad*   **de l'**eau *some water*

Grammaire

- **du, de la, de l', des** are sometimes used when we don't say 'some' in English:
  Je voudrais **des** frites.
  I'd like chips or *I'd like some chips.*

A2.4 mon, ton, son, etc. my, your, his/her

- The word for 'my' depends on whether the noun it is used with is masculine or feminine, singular or plural.

masculine singular	feminine singular	masculine and feminine plural
mon	ma	mes

mon frère	**ma** sœur	**mes** parents
my brother	*my sister*	*my parents*

- The word for 'your' also depends on whether the noun it is used with is masculine or feminine, singular or plural.

masculine singular	feminine singular	masculine and feminine plural
ton	ta	tes

ton frère	**ta** sœur	**tes** parents
your brother	*your sister*	*your parents*

- The word for 'his' and 'her' is the same. It depends on whether the noun it is used with is masculine or feminine, singular or plural.

masculine singular	feminine singular	masculine and feminine plural
son	sa	ses

son frère	**sa** sœur	**ses** parents
his brother,	*his sister,*	*his parents,*
her brother	*her sister*	*her parents*

J'aime David Beckham. J'adore **ses** vêtements.
*I like David Beckham. I like **his** clothes.*

J'adore Avril Lavigne. J'aime **sa** musique.
*I love Avril Lavigne. I like **her** music.*

A2.5 ce, cette, cet this, ces these

- The words for 'this' and 'these' depend on whether the noun that follows is masculine or feminine, singular or plural.

	masculine singular*	feminine singular*		masculine and femine plural
this	ce	**cette**	*these*	ces
if a masculine noun starts with a vowel or a silent h				
cet				

ce livre *this book*
cette bague *this ring*
ces bonbons *these sweets*
cet appareil-photo *this camera*

A2.6 Summary of determiners

	masculine singular	feminine singular	masculine and feminine plural
the	le	la	les
a	un	une	*(not applicable)*
some	du	de la	des
my	mon	ma	mes
your	ton	ta	tes
his, her	son	sa	ses
this, these	ce	cette	ces

A3 Les adjectifs Adjectives

A3.1 Masculine/feminine, singular/plural adjectives

- Adjectives are words that describe nouns. The basic rules in French are:
  - add an **-e** to the adjective if the noun it describes is feminine singular
  - add an **-s** to the adjective if the noun it describes is masculine plural
  - add **-es** to the adjective if the noun it describes is feminine plural

	masculine	feminine
singular	mon petit frère	ma petit**e** sœur
plural	mes petit**s** frères	mes petit**es** sœurs

- Adjectives that end in -e anyway don't take a second -e in the feminine:
  (masc. sing.) Il est timide. *He is shy.*
  (fem. sing.) Elle est timide. *She is shy.*

- But adjectives that end in -é <u>do</u> take a second -e in the feminine:
  (masc. sing.) il est **marié** *he is married*
  (fem. sing.) elle est **mariée** *she is married*

- Here are some special cases:

	masculine singular	feminine singular
white	blanc	blan**che**
sporty	sportif	sport**ive**
good-looking	beau	**belle**
boring	ennuyeux	ennuy**euse**
lazy	paresseux	paress**euse**
happy	heureux	heur**euse**
musical	musicien	music**ienne**
brown	marron	marron
nice	sympa	sympa

elle est **sportive** *she is sporty*
ma sœur est **sympa** *my sister is nice*

- Where an adjective describes a group including masculine and feminine, use the masculine form of the adjective:

  Les élèves sont **bruyants**.
  The pupils (boys and girls) are noisy.

A3.2 The position of adjectives

- **petit** (small), **grand** (big), **vieux** (old) and **beau** (beautiful) come before the noun, as in English:

  un **petit** village *a small village*
  une **grande** ville *a big town*
  un **vieux** village *an old village*
  une **belle** ville *a beautiful town*

- Other adjectives come <u>after</u> the noun they describe:

  un château **intéressant** *an interesting castle*
  une ville **historique** *a historic town*

B Verbs

B1 The present tense of regular verbs

- French verbs take different endings according to <u>who</u> is doing the action.

The regular pattern is as follows:

verb: **regarder** *to watch*

je	-e	je regard**e**	*I watch, I'm watching*
tu	-es	tu regard**es**	*you watch, you're watching*
il elle on	-e	il regard**e** elle regard**e** on regard**e**	*he watches, he's watching* *she watches, she's watching* *we/they watch, are watching*
nous	-ons	nous regard**ons**	*we watch, we're watching*
vous	-ez	vous regard**ez**	*you watch, you're watching*
ils elles	-ent	ils regard**ent** elles regard**ent**	*they (boys) watch, they're watching* *they (girls) watch, they're watching*

For use of *tu, on, il,* etc. see Section C below.

- *regarde, regardes, regardent* are all pronounced the same.

- Singular nouns take the same endings as *il / elle*:
  Ma mère travaille. *My mother works.*

- Plural nouns take the same endings as *ils / elles*:
  Les pompiers arrivent. *The firefighters arrive.*

- Other verbs that follow this pattern include:

j'adore *I love*	j'habite *I live*
j'aime *I like*	j'invite *I invite*
j'arrive *I arrive*	je joue *I play*
je bavarde *I chat*	je lave *I wash*
je chante *I sing*	je loue *I hire*
je déjeune *I have lunch*	je mange *I eat*
je déteste *I hate*	je parle *I talk*
je dîne *I have my evening meal*	je quitte *I leave*
je donne *I give*	je reste *I stay*
j'écoute *I listen (to)*	je surfe *I surf*
je ferme *I close*	je travaille *I work*
je gagne *I win*	je trouve *I find*
	je visite *I visit*

Tu aimes le tennis? – Oui, j'aime le tennis.
Do you like tennis? – Yes, I like tennis.
Vous habitez à Paris? – Non, nous habitons à Boulogne.
Do you live in Paris? – No, we live in Boulogne.

B2 Reflexive verbs

- Reflexive verbs have an extra part between the pronoun and the verb:

  je **me** lève *I get up*   je **m**'appelle *I am called*
  tu **te** lèves *you get up*   tu **t**'appelles *you are called*

B3 The present tense of irregular verbs

- The following verbs don't follow the regular verb pattern described in Section B1 above.

B3.1 avoir to have

j'	**ai**	*I have*	nous	**avons**	*we have*
tu	**as**	*you have*	vous	**avez**	*you have*
il	**a**	*he has*	ils	**ont**	*they have*
elle	**a**	*she has*	elles	**ont**	*they have*

Tu as un animal? *Do you have a pet?*

- J'ai means 'I have'. But in these phrases, it means 'I am':

  j'ai 14 ans *I am 14*
  j'ai faim *I am hungry*
  j'ai soif *I am thirsty*

B3.2 être to be

je	**suis**	*I am*	nous	**sommes**	*we are*
tu	**es**	*you are*	vous	**êtes**	*you are*
il	**est**	*he is*	ils	**sont**	*they are*
elle	**est**	*she is*	elles	**sont**	*they are*

Je suis française. *I am French.*

Grammaire

B3.3 *aller* to go

je **vais** *I go, I'm going*	nous **allons** *we go, we're going*
tu **vas** *you go, you're going*	vous **allez** *you go, you're going*
il **va** *he goes, he's going*	ils **vont** *they go, they're going*
elle **va** *she goes, she's going*	elles **vont** *they go, they're going*

Je vais en France en juin. *I'm going to France in June.*

● Use **aller** and the infinitive to say what people are going to do in the future (see Section B7).

● The past tense is: **je suis allé** *I went (male)*, **je suis allée** *I went (female)* (see Section B4.3).

B3.4 *faire* to do

je **fais** *I do, I'm doing*	nous **faisons** *we do, we're doing*
tu **fais** *you do, you're doing*	vous **faites** *you do, you're doing*
il **fait** *he does, he's doing*	ils **font** *they do, they're doing*
elle **fait** *she does, she's doing*	elles **font** *they do, they're doing*

● The verb **faire** has a range of meanings, depending on the noun it is used with:

Je fais de la natation. *I **go** swimming.*
Mes copains font du judo. *My friends **do** judo.*
On a fait un pique-nique. *We **had** a picnic.*

● **Faire** is also used in expressions with weather:
il fait mauvais *the weather's bad*

B3.5 Some other irregular verbs

pouvoir + infinitive **can**		vouloir + infinitive **to want to**	
je **peux**	*I can*	je **veux**	*I want to*
tu **peux**	*you can*	tu **veux**	*you want to*
il/elle **peut**	*he/she can*	il/elle **veut**	*he/she wants to*

devoir + infinitive **must**		boire **to drink**	
je **dois**	*I must*	je **bois**	*I drink*
tu **dois**	*you must*	tu **bois**	*you drink*
il/elle **doit**	*he/she must*	il/elle **boit**	*he/she drinks*

B4 *Le passé* The perfect tense/past tense

● The perfect tense consists of <u>two</u> parts:

	1 auxiliary verb	2 past participle	
j'	**ai**	**joué**	au rugby *I played rugby*
elle	**a**	**regardé**	la télé *she watched TV*
je	**suis**	**allé(e)**	en ville *I went to town*

● The first part, the *auxiliary verb*, is usually **avoir** (**j'ai, tu as, il a,** etc.), but it can be **être** (**je suis, tu es,** etc.).

● The second part, the *past participle*, often ends in -**é**: the -**é** <u>is</u> pronounced.

● The past tense in French can have <u>two</u> meanings in English:

il a divorcé can mean *he divorced* OR *he has divorced*.

B4.1 The past tense of regular verbs with avoir

● Examples of regular verbs are listed in Section B1 above.

● The auxiliary verb is **avoir** (**j'ai, tu as, il/elle a, nous avons,** etc. – see Section B3.1).

● The past participle is formed by replacing the verb ending with -**é**.

present   past
je joue   j̶e̶'ai jou̶e̶ é   j'ai joué
I play   *I played*

Hier, on a regardé un film.
Yesterday we watched a film.

À midi, j'**ai** mangé un hot-dog.
At midday I ate a hot-dog.

B4.2 The past tense of irregular verbs with avoir

● The auxiliary verb is **avoir** (**j'ai, tu as, il/elle a, nous avons,** etc. – see Section B3.1).

● The past participle is unpredictable and has to be learnt.

verb	past tense
faire *to do*	j'ai **fait** *I did*
avoir *to have*	j'ai **eu** *I had*
boire *to drink*	j'ai **bu** *I drank*
lire *to read*	j'ai **lu** *I read*
voir *to see*	j'ai **vu** *I saw*
perdre *to lose*	j'ai **perdu** *I lost*
vomir *to be sick*	j'ai **vomi** *I was sick*

B4.3 The past tense of verbs with être

- A few verbs have the auxiliary **je suis** (not **j'ai**). The most common is **je suis allé** (I went).

- Unlike verbs that take **j'ai**, you add an **-e** to the past participle for females:

    (male) je suis allé *(female)* je suis all**é**e

    Lundi dernier, je suis all**é** en ville.
    Last Monday, I went into town. (said by a male)
    Lundi dernier, je suis all**é**e en ville.
    Last Monday, I went into town. (said by a female)
    On est allé à la mer.
    We went to the seaside.

B4.4 Special case: c'était

- **C'était** means 'it was' or 'it used to be':

    L'excursion, c'était amusant.
    The trip was fun.

B5 Telling people what to do (the imperative)

B5.1 Speaking to someone of your own age

- To people with whom you would say **tu** (see Section C2 below), use the verb ending in **-e**:
    écoute les dialogues *listen to the dialogues*

- Some irregular verbs have an **-s** ending:
    écris une lettre *write a letter*

B5.2 Speaking to more than one person, or to an adult not in your family

- To people with whom you would say **vous** (see Section C2 below), use the verb with the **vous** endings:
    (vous descendez *you get off*) **Descendez** à la gare.
                                                     Get off at the station.

B6 The infinitive

- The infinitive is the 'name' of the verb – the form you find in a dictionary. Unlike the forms used after *je, il,* etc. (*je fais, il fait,* etc.), the infinitive never changes.

- The infinitive of regular verbs ends in **-er**.
    The infinitive of other verbs ends in **-ir** or **-re**.
    jouer *to play* **finir** *to finish* **lire** *to read*

- Use the infinitive after the following verbs:
    j'aime *I like*   je dois *I have to*   je déteste *I hate*
    je peux *I can*   je veux *I want to*   je préfère *I prefer*
    on peut *you can*
        J'aime **danser**. *I like dancing.*
        On peut **faire** du surf. *You can go surfing.*

B7 The future

- Use **aller** and the infinitive to say what people are going to do in the future:
    Je **vais rester** chez moi. *I'm going to stay at home.*
    On **va aller** en France. *We're going to go to France.*

C Pronouns

C1 *je* I

- **je** and **j'** both mean 'I'. Use **j'** if the word that follows begins with *h* or a vowel:

    Je regarde la télé. *I watch TV.*
    J'ai une sœur. *I have a sister.*

C2 *tu, vous*: two words for 'you'

- Use **tu** when you're talking to someone (one person) of your own age or someone in the family.

- Use **vous** when you're talking to an adult (one person) not in your family, e.g. your teacher.

- Use **vous**, also, when talking to more than one person – whatever their age, whether or not you know them well.

    Tu as un bic, s'il te plaît, Marie?
    Do you have a biro, please, Marie?
    Vous avez un livre, s'il vous plaît, madame?
    Do you have a book, please, Miss?
    Vous travaillez, Karen et Michael?
    Are you working, Karen and Michael?

C3 *moi, toi* me, you (after prepositions)

- avec **moi** *with me*   avec **toi** *with you*
    chez **moi** *at my house*   chez **toi** *at your house*

C4 *il, elle* he, she

- **il** usually means 'he'; **elle** means 'she'.
    Il a 11 ans, et **elle** a 15 ans.
    He's 11 years old, and she's 15 years old.

- **il** can mean 'it', referring to a masculine noun; **elle** can mean 'it', referring to a feminine noun:
    J'aime ma maison. **Elle** est grande.
    *I like my house. **It** is big.*

- **il** is also used in set expressions:
    – **il y a** *there is, there are*
        Il y a des cafés en ville. *There are cafés in town.*
    – weather expressions
        il pleut *it rains, it is raining*

Grammaire

C5 *on* we, they, people

- **on** takes the same part of the verb as *il/elle*.

- **on** can mean 'we', and can be used instead of *nous*:

    On a joué aux cartes. *We played cards.*

- **on** can also mean 'people generally' (in English, we often say 'they' or 'you'):

    On peut louer des vélos.
    You can hire bikes.

C6 *nous* we

- **nous** means 'we':

    Nous allons au centre commercial.
    We go to the shopping centre.

C7 *ils, elles* they

- **ils** = *they* (all male, or mixed group of males and females)
  elles = *they* (female)

    Tes parents aiment la musique? – Oui, **ils** aiment beaucoup la musique.
    Do your parents like music? – Yes, they like music a lot.

D Prepositions

D1 *à: au, à la, aux*

D1.1 *à*

- **à** can mean:
  - *in*   J'habite **à** Paris. *I live in Paris.*
  - *at*   J'arrive **à** une heure. *I arrive at one o'clock.*
  - *to*   Je vais **à** Londres. *I'm going to London*
    (for 'to' + *countries*, see Section D3 below)

- Some special expressions:
  - à pied *on foot*, à vélo *by bike*
  - une glace à trois boules *an ice cream with three scoops*
  - l'équipe a gagné 3 à 0 *the team won 3-0*

D1.2 *au, à la, à l', aux* to the, at the

- **à** + **le** <u>always</u> combine to form the one word **au**.
  à + **les** <u>always</u> combine to form the one word **aux**.
  à + **la** and **à** + **l'** are fine.

with masculine nouns	with feminine nouns
je vais **au** collège	tu vas **à la** plage?
I go to school	*do you go to the beach?*

if the singular noun begins with a vowel or silent *h*
je suis allé **à l'**hôpital *I went to hospital*

with all plural nouns
il va **aux** halles *he's going to the covered market*

- **au** is also used
  - with flavours and fillings:
      un gâteau **au** chocolat *a chocolate cake*
  - with sports:
      Je joue **au** basket. *I play basketball.*

- **au, à la, à l', aux** are also used to talk about aches and pains: j'ai mal...
  au + masculine noun:
  J'ai mal au dos. *I have a bad back.*
  à la + feminine noun:
  J'ai mal à la main. *I have a sore hand.*
  à l' if the noun begins with vowel:
  J'ai mal à l'estomac. *I have stomach ache.*
  aux + masc. or fem. plural noun:
  J'ai mal aux pieds. *I have sore feet.*

D2 *de: du, de la, des*

- **de** can mean 'of'. Shorten **de** to **d'** before *h* or a vowel:

    la chambre **de** ma sœur (*the room of my sister* =)
    my sister's room
    le prof **d'**histoire (*the teacher of history* =)
    the history teacher

- **de** is used with <u>quantities</u> of food:

    un paquet **de** chips *a packet of crisps*

(For 'some', use **du / de la / des** – see Section A2.3 above.)

- **de** is sometimes part of other expressions:

près de *near*	J'habite **près de** Calais.
	I live near Calais.
beaucoup de *lots of*	Il y a **beaucoup de** violence.
	There is a lot of violence.
trop de *too much* *too many*	Il y a **trop de** gros mots.
	There is too much bad language.
de... à ... *from... to...*	**de** 10h00 à 18h00
	from 10 am to 6 pm

D2.1 *du, de la, de l', des* of the

- **de** + **le** <u>always</u> combine to form the one word **du**.
  de + **les** <u>always</u> combine to form the one word **des**:
  de + **la** and **de** + **l'** are fine.

  Use this pattern:
- with **jouer** + musical instruments:
    Je joue **du** piano. *I play the piano.*
    Je joue **de la** guitare. *I play the guitar.*

- with activities and the verb **faire**:
    On fait **du** surf. *We go surfing.*

Grammaire

D3 Prepositions with countries

- The same preposition means 'in' and 'to' a country.

	masculine singular	feminine singular	all plural countries
in or to + country	**au** Brésil	**en** France	**aux** États-Unis

J'habite en Grande-Bretagne.
I live in Great Britain.

D4 More prepositions

at	à + precise time	J'arrive au collège à 8h40. *I arrive at school at 8.40.*
	vers + vague time	Nous allons rentrer vers 20h00. *We'll return at about 8 pm.*
	le + weekend	Je fais mes devoirs le week-end. *I do my homework at the weekend.*
	chez (at …'s house)	On se retrouve chez moi? *Shall we meet at my house?*
by	à + bike	Je vais au collège à vélo. *I go to school by bike.*
	en + other transport	Tu vas en bus ou en auto? *Are you going by bus or by car?*
in	à + named town	J'habite à Birmingham. *I live in Birmingham.*
	dans + club	Je joue dans l'orchestre. *I play in the orchestra.*
	dans + direction	C'est dans le nord. *It's in the north.*
	en + language	Nous avons bavardé en anglais. *We chatted in English.*
	en + month	en août *in August*
	en, au + season	en hiver, été, automne *in winter, summer, autumn* au printemps *in spring*
near	près de	C'est près du parc. *It's near the park.*
on	sur	Je surfe sur Internet. *I surf (on) the internet.*
	à + pied	Je vais au collège à pied. *I go to school on foot.*
to	à + named town	Je vais à Nice. *I'm going to Nice.*
	en + ville	Le week-end, je vais en ville. *At the weekend, I go to town.*
	'to a country'	see D3 above
	chez + people	Il va chez sa tante. *He's going to his aunt's.*
	'to the'	see D1.2 above
with		Il sort avec Léa.
	avec + person	*He's going out with Léa.*

E Shaping and linking sentences

E1 Negative sentences

- The basic rule is: to make a sentence negative, put **ne** before the verb and **pas** after it:

Il fait froid. — Il **ne** fait **pas** froid.
It's cold. — *It isn't cold.*

- Shorten **ne** to **n'** if the word that follows begins with *h* or a vowel:

J'aime le fromage. — Je **n'**aime **pas** le fromage.
I like cheese. — *I don't like cheese.*
C'est vrai. — Ce **n'**est **pas** vrai.
It's true. — *It isn't true.*

- In negative sentences, **un** and **une** are replaced with **de**:

J'ai un frère; je n'ai pas **de** sœur.
I have a brother; I don't have a sister.

- Here are some other negative expressions:

ne (verb) **jamais** *never*	il **ne** fume **jamais** *he never smokes*
ne (verb) **personne** *no-one*	il **n'**y a **personne** *there is no-one*

E2 Questions

- You can ask questions simply by making your voice go higher at the end of the sentence:

Tu as un bic. *You have a pen.*
Tu as un bic? *Do you have a pen?*

- You can start the question with **est-ce que**:

Tu as un bic. *You have a pen.*
Est-ce que tu as un bic? *Do you have a pen?*

- Or you can invert the subject and the verb:
As-tu un bic? *Do you have a pen?*

- Many questions contain special question words:

combien *how much*	C'est combien? *How much is it?*
comment *how*	Ça s'écrit comment? *How do you spell it?*
comment *what*	Comment t'appelles-tu? *What are you called*
où *where*	Où habites-tu? *Where do you live?*
pourquoi *why*	Tu aimes les jeux? Pourquoi? *Do you like games shows? Why?*
quand *when*	C'est quand, ton anniversaire? *When's your birthday?*
quel (m) *which, what*	Quel temps fait-il? *What's the weather like?*
quelle (f) *which, what*	C'est quelle photo? *Which photo is it?* À quelle heure? *At what time?*
qu'est-ce que *what*	Qu'est-ce que tu aimes? *What do you like?*
qui *who*	Tu joues au tennis avec qui? *Who do you play tennis with?*
quoi *what*	Ta couleur préférée, c'est quoi? *What's your favourite colour?*

Grammaire

E3 Linking sentences

- Use the following words to link shorter sentences together to make longer ones:

et *and*	Je suis anglaise et j'habite à York. *I'm English and I live in York.*
et puis *and then*	Nous dînons et puis nous sortons. *We have our evening meal and then we go out.*
mais *but*	J'aime l'eau mais je n'aime pas le lait. *I like water but I don't like milk.*
ou *or*	Je vais à la piscine ou je fais du vélo. *I go to the swimming pool or I go cycling.*
parce que *because*	J'aime *Le Bigdil* parce que c'est amusant. *I like* Le Bigdil *because it's funny.*

E4 Qualifiers

- Use the following to make what you say more precise:

très *very*	Il fait **très** chaud. *It's very hot.*
vraiment *really*	Il fait **vraiment** froid. *It's really cold.*
assez *quite*	Elle est **assez** sportive. *She is quite sporty.*
souvent *often*	Il est **souvent** paresseux. *He is often lazy.*
parfois *sometimes*	Je suis **parfois** impertinent(e). *I am sometimes cheeky.*
toujours *always*	Il est **toujours** heureux. *He is always happy.*

E5 Word order

- Adjectives usually come after the nouns they describe:
des CD vierges *blank CDs*

  grand, petit, vieux and *beau* are exceptions:
une petite ville *a small town*

- The French word order is often the reverse of English:

la télé-réalité	*reality TV*
une émission de sport	*a sports programme*
la salle à manger	*the dining room*

F Numbers, time, frequency

F1 Numbers

1 un	6 six	11 onze	16 seize
2 deux	7 sept	12 douze	17 dix-sept
3 trois	8 huit	13 treize	18 dix-huit
4 quatre	9 neuf	14 quatorze	19 dix-neuf
5 cinq	10 dix	15 quinze	20 vingt

20 vingt	60 soixante	100 cent
30 trente	70 soixante-dix	1000 mille
40 quarante	80 quatre-vingts	1000 000 un million
50 cinquante	90 quatre-vingt-dix	

21 vingt **et** un	51 cinquante **et** un	81 quatre-vingt-un
31 trente **et** un	61 soixante **et** un	91 quatre-vingt-onze
41 quarante **et** un	71 soixante **et** onze	101 cent un

25 vingt-cinq	65 soixante-cinq
35 trente-cinq	75 soixante-quinze
45 quarante-cinq	85 quatre-vingt-cinq
55 cinquante-cinq	95 quatre-vingt-quinze
	105 cent cinq

- *quatre-vingts* (80) has an *-s*. Linked with other numbers, it hasn't: *quatre-vingt-un, quatre-vingt-deux,* etc.

- Ordinal numbers are as follows:

1st = 1er premier *m*, 1ère première *f*	4th = 4ème le/la quatrième (note the e in *quatre* is dropped)
2nd = 2ème le/la deuxième	
3rd = 3ème le/la troisième	5th = 5ème le/la cinquième

F2 Days and dates

- Use the usual numbers in dates (and no word for 'of'):
le trois avril *the third of April*

- Exception: use **le premier** for the first of the month:
le premier mai *the first of May*

- Days and months don't have capitals in French.

F3 Time

- The 24-hour clock is written as follows:
à treize heures quarante (13h40) *at thirteen-forty*

- The 12-hour clock is written as follows:
  il est deux heures cinq *it's five past two*
  il est deux heures et quart *it's a quarter past two*
  il est deux heures vingt-cinq *it's twenty-five past two*
  il est deux heures et demie *it's half-past two*
  il est trois heures moins vingt *it's twenty to three*
  il est trois heures moins le quart *it's a quarter to three*
  il est trois heures moins dix *it's ten to three*
  il est trois heures *it's three o'clock*

- Note: il est midi *it's midday*, il est minuit *it's midnight*

F4 When and how often

- There is no word for 'in' the evening, 'on' Saturday, or 'at' the weekend:

le soir *in the evening*	**le week-end** *at the weekend*
le samedi après-midi *on Saturday afternoons*	

- To say how often you do an activity, use:

parfois *sometimes*	Je vais parfois au parc. *I sometimes go to the park.*
souvent *often*	On va souvent à la mer. *We often go to the sea.*
toujours *always*	Je déjeune toujours à midi. *I always have lunch at midday.*

Stratégies! *Using the glossary*

Words are in alphabetical order. To find a word, look up its first letter, then find it according to the alphabetical order of its second and third letters: e.g. **école** comes before **été** because **éc-** comes before **ét-**.

A

à 1 *in:* j'habite à Lyon *I live in Lyons*
2 *away:* c'est à 10 minutes *it's 10 minutes away*
3 *on:* à la télé *on TV*
4 *to:* à la mer *to the seaside*
5 *from:* à partir de 14h *from 2pm*
6 *with:* à deux boules *with two scoops*
7 *at:* à dix heures *at ten o'clock*
à + = à plus tard *see you later*
à bientôt *see you soon*
à mon avis *in my opinion*
à pied *on foot*
à samedi *see you on Saturday*
à ton tour *your turn*
a *has*
elle a un frère *she has a brother*
il a 14 ans *he's 14 years old*
accident *m accident*
acheté *bought*
j'ai acheté *I bought*
acheter *to buy*
j'achète *I buy*
acteur *m* **actrice** *f actor*
actif *m,* **active** *f active*
la plus active *the most active*
action *f action*
activité *f activity*
actrice *f actress*
adapter *to adapt*
adjectif *m adjective*
adorent *adore*
j'adore *I love*
ils, elles adorent *they adore*
adorer *to love, adore*
adresse *f address*
c'est quoi, ton adresse e-mail? *what is your e-mail address?*
adulte *m or f adult*
aéroport *m airport*
Afrique *f Africa*
âge *m age*
quel âge as-tu? *how old are you?*
il a quel âge? *how old is he?*
à l'âge de 18 ans *at the age of 18*
agenda *m diary*
ai *have*
j'ai *I have (from avoir)*
je n'ai pas de *I don't have a*
aider *to help*
aïe! *ouch!*
aime *like*
j'aime *I like*
je n'aime pas *I don't like*
aimé *liked, loved*
j'ai beaucoup aimé… *I liked … a lot*
aimer *to like, love*
tu aimes la télé-réalité? *do you like reality TV?*
ajouter *to add*
album de photos *m photo album*
alcool *m alcohol*
il boit beaucoup d'alcool *he drinks a lot*
alerté *called*
j'ai alerté la police *I called the police*

allé *went*
je suis allé *m,* je suis allée *f I went (past tense of aller)*
il est allé *he went*
elle est allée *she went*
ils sont allés *they went*
Allemagne *f Germany*
allemand *m,* **allemande** *f German*
aller *to go*
je vais aller *I'm going to go*
on va aller *we're going to go*
allô! *hello! (on the phone)*
alors 1 *well then* 2 *so*
alternatif *m,* **alternative** *f alternative*
amant *m,* **amante** *f lover*
ambition *f ambition*
ambulance *f ambulance*
américain *m,* **américaine** *f American*
Amérique du Sud *f South America*
ami *m,* **amie** *f friend*
amusant *m,* **amusante** *f amusing, funny*
ce n'est pas amusant ça! *that's no joke!*
amusé: on s'est bien amusé *we enjoyed ourselves*
an *m year*
par an *per year*
j'ai 14 ans *I'm 14 years old*
anglais *m,* **anglaise** *f English*
Angleterre *f England*
animal *m animal*
animaux *mpl animals*
animé (par) *presented (by)*
année *f year*
l'année prochaine *next year*
l'année dernière *last year*
anniversaire *m birthday*
c'est quand, ton anniversaire? *when's your birthday?*
bonne anniversaire! *happy birthday!*
annoncer *to announce*
ans: j'ai 14 ans *I'm 14 years old*
anxieux *m,* **anxieuse** *f anxious*
je suis anxieuse *I'm anxious*
août *August*
en août *in August*
appareil-photo *m camera*
appartement *m flat, apartment*
appelé *called*
j'ai appelé un taxi *I called a taxi*
appeler *to call, name*
comment t'appelles-tu? *what's your name?*
qui s'appelle *who is called*
après *after*
après le collège *after school*
après-midi *m afternoon*
archinul: c'est archinul *it's complete rubbish*
armé *m,* **armée** *f armed*
arobase *m @ (in e-mail address)*
arrêté *arrested*
la police a arrêté *the police arrested*
arrêter *to stop*
arrivé *arrived*
je suis arrivé *m,* je suis arrivée *f I arrived*
elle est arrivée *she arrived*
ils sont arrivés *they arrived*

article *m article*
artiste *m or f artist*
as *have (from avoir)*
tu as un frère? *do you have a brother?*
tu as quel âge? *how old are you?*
assez 1 *quite:* assez bien *quite good,* assez facile *quite easy*
2 assez de *enough*
attaché *attached*
il s'est attaché *he attached himself*
attendre *to wait (for)*
attente *f wait*
8 heures d'attente *8 hours' wait*
attraction *f attraction*
au 1 *to the, at the*
du 01/10 au 30/04 *from 1st October to 30th April*
je joue au volley *I play volleyball*
2 *in, to:* au Canada *in Canada*
au pôle Nord/Sud *in the North/South Pole*
au printemps *in spring*
au sud de Lyon *to the south of Lyon*
au revoir *good-bye*
auberge de jeunesse *f youth hostel*
audition *f audition*
aujourd'hui *today*
aussi *also*
Australie *f Australia*
australien *m,* **australienne** *f Australian*
auto *f car*
en auto *by car*
autos tamponneuses *bumper cars*
automne *m autumn*
en automne *in autumn*
autre *m or f other*
note d'autres détails *note other details*
l'autre *the other one*
aux *pl to the*
réponds aux questions *answer the questions*
avait: il y avait *there was*
avant *before*
avec *with*
avec qui? *with whom?*
aventure *f adventure*
avez: vous avez *you (pl) have (from avoir)*
avis *m opinion*
avoir *to have*
avons: nous avons *we have (from avoir)*
avril *April*
en avril *in April*

B

badminton *m badminton*
bague *f ring (for finger)*
baguette *f French stick (bread)*
ballon *m ball*
banane *f* 1 *banana* 2 *bum-bag*
bande dessinée *f comic strip*
banque *f bank*
barbant *m,* **barbante** *f boring*
barbare *m or f barbaric*
barbe à papa *f candy floss*
barbecue *m barbecue*
faire un barbecue *to have a barbecue*

Glossaire français–anglais

bas *m*, **basse** *f* *down*
basilique *f* *basilica*
   la Basilique Saint-Pierre *St Peter's Basilica (in Rome)*
basket *m* *basketball*
   je joue au basket *I play basketball*
bateau *m* *boat*
bateau renverseur *m* *swing boat (funfair ride)*
batterie *f* *battery*
   l'élevage en batterie *battery farming*
battu *beaten*
   battu à mort *beaten to death*
bavard *m*, **bavarde** *f* *chatty, talkative*
bavardé *chatted*
   j'ai bavardé avec *I chatted with*
beau *m*, **belle** *f* *good-looking*
   il fait beau *the weather is fine*
beaucoup (de) *lots of, many*
   il, elle a beaucoup de talent *he, she has lots of talent*
   j'aime beaucoup le lait *I like milk a lot*
bébé *m* *baby*
belge *m or f* *Belgian*
Belgique *f* *Belgium*
belle *f* *good-looking, beautiful*
ben *well*
berk! *yuk!*
bête *m* 1 *animal*: des bêtes en liberté *animals in the wild* 2 *m or f* *stupid*
beurre *f* *butter*
bibliothèque *f* *library*
bic *m* *biro*
bien 1 *well*: il a bien joué *he played well* 2 *good, fine, OK*
   très bien *very good*
   bien sûr *of course*
   oui, j'aime bien *yes, I like it*
   ça va bien *I'm fine*
   c'était bien *it was good*
bientôt *soon*
   à bientôt! *see, hear from you soon!*
bière *f* *beer*
biscuits *mpl* *biscuits*
blague *f* *joke*
blanc *m*, **blanche** *f* *white*
blazer *m* *blazer*
bleu *m*, **bleue** *f* *blue*
bloc-notes *m* *notepad*
bof! *so-so!*
boire *to drink*
boit *drinks*
   il, elle boit *he, she drinks (from boire)*
   elle boit beaucoup d'alcool *she drinks a lot*
bon appétit! *enjoy your meal!*
bon *m*, **bonne** *f* *good, right*
   dans le bon ordre *in the right order*
bonbons *mpl* *sweets*
bonjour! *hello!*
   bonjour à ta famille *say hello to your family for me*
bonne *f* *good*
   bonne anniversaire *happy birthday*
   la bonne option *the right option*
   bonne idée *good idea*
   de bonne qualité *good quality*
boucherie *f* *butcher's*
boulangerie *f* *baker's*
boutique *f* *shop*
bouton *m* *button*
bowling *m* *bowling alley*
boxe *f* *boxing*
bras *m* *arm*
   j'ai mal au bras *my arm hurts*
brésilien *m*, **brésilienne** *f* *Brazilian*
britannique *m or f* *British*

brochure *f* *brochure*
brouhaha *m* *hustle and bustle*
Bruxelles *Brussels*
bu *drank*
   on a bu *we drank*
bureau *m* *office*
bus *m* *bus*
   en bus *by bus*

C

ça *that*
   ça va? *how are you?*
   ça va bien *I'm fine*
   je n'aime pas ça *I don't like that*
   ça dépend *it depends*
   j'aime ça *I like that*
   ça s'écrit comment? *how do you spell it?*
câble *m* *cable (TV)*
cadeau *m* (*pl* cadeaux) *present*
café *m* 1 *café*: au café *in a café* 2 *coffee*
cahier *m* *exercise book*
cage *f* *cage*
calculatrice *f* *calculator*
campagne *f* *countryside*
Canada *m* *Canada*
cantine *f* *canteen*
canadien *m*, **canadienne** *f* *Canadian*
candidat *m* *candidate*
canoë *canoeing*
   je fais du canoë *I go canoeing*
cantine *f* *canteen*
capitale *f* *capital (city)*
captivité *f* *captivity*
   en captivité *in captivity*
car *m* *coach*
caractère *m* *personality*
   trait de caractère *personality trait*
carnivore *m or f* *carnivorous*
carottes *fpl* *carrots*
carré *square*
   deux mille kilomètres carrés *2000 km²*
carte *f* 1 *card*: carte postale *postcard*
   carte téléphonique *phone card*
   on joue aux cartes *we play cards* 2 *map*
casque *m* *helmet*
cassis *m* *blackcurrant*
cathédrale *f* *cathedral*
cause *f* *cause*
CD *m* *CD*
ce *m* 1 *this*: ce week-end *this weekend* 2 *it*: ce n'est pas important *it's not important*
   ce sont quels mots? *which words are they?*
   c'est vrai *it's true*
   ce n'est pas vrai *it's not true*
célèbre *m or f* *famous*
célébrité *f* *celebrity*
cellule *f* *cell*
   cellules nerveuses *nerve cells*
cent 100
   cent grammes *100g*
   pour cent *per cent*
centime *m* *cent (100 cents = 1 euro)*
centre *m* *centre*
   au centre *in the centre*
   centre commercial *shopping centre*
   centre sportif *sports centre*
céréales *fpl* *cereal*
certificat *m* *certificate*
c'est *it's, is it…?*
   c'est combien *how much is it?*
   c'est fait *it's done*
   c'est vrai *it's true*
   c'est qui, ta star préférée? *who is your favourite film/sports star?*

c'était *it was*
   c'était bien *it was good*
   c'était le top *it was great*
   c'était nul *it was rubbish*
cette *f* *this*
chaîne de télé *f* *TV channel*
chambre *f* *bedroom*
   chambre d'hôtel *hotel room*
changé *changed*
   ils ont changé de train *they changed trains*
changer *to change*
chanson *f* *song*
chanté *sang*
   il, elle a chanté *he, she sang*
chanter *to sing*
chanteur *m*, **chanteuse** *f* *singer*
chaque *each*
charcuterie *f* *delicatessen*
chasse *f* *hunting*
chat *m* *cat*
château *m* (*pl* châteaux) *castle*
chaud *m*, **chaude** *f* *hot*
   il fait chaud *the weather is hot*
cher *m*, **chère** *f* 1 *dear* 2 *expensive*: ça ne doit pas coûter cher! *it mustn't be expensive!*
chéri *m*, **chérie** *f* *darling*
cheval *m* *horse*
   faire du cheval *to go horseriding*
chez *at or to the house of*
   chez le docteur *to the doctor's*
   chez les Cassou *at the Cassous' (house)*
   chez mon cousin *to my cousin's house*
chien *m* *dog*
chiffre *m* *number, figure*
chips *fpl* *crisps*
   un paquet de chips *a bag of crisps*
chocolat *m* *chocolate*
choisis *choose*
   choisis le bon mot *choose the right word*
choix *m* *choice*
chose *f* *thing*
   choses à manger *things to eat*
chronologique: ordre chronologique *chronological order*
cigarette *f* *cigarette*
cinéma *m* *cinema*
cinq *five*
cinquante *fifty*
cirque *m* *circus*
citron *m* *lemon*
classe *f* *class*
classique *m or f* *classical*
climat *m* *climate*
cliquer sur *to click on*
coca *m* *coke*
cocher *to tick*
collège *m* *school*
colline *f* *hill*
Colisée *f* *Coliseum (in Rome)*
combien (de)? *how much, many?*
   c'est combien *how much is it?*
comédie *f* *comedy show*
comique *m* *comedian*
commande *f* *order*
comme *like, such as*
commencer *to begin*
comment *how*
   comment t'appelles tu? *what is your name?*
   le restaurant est comment? *what is the restaurant like?*
   ça s'écrit comment? *how do you spell it?*
commentée *with a commentary*
   une visite commentée *a tour with a commentary*
complet *m*, **complète** *f* *complete*
compléter *to complete*
   complète *complete*

compositeur m **compositrice** f composer
compris: **je n'ai pas compris** I haven't understood
concert m concert
connaissance f knowledge
il fait la connaissance de he meets
consulte la page 41 look at page 41
continué continued
on a continué (à) we continued
contraire m opposite
contre against
je suis contre les zoos I'm against zoos
conversation f conversation
coordonnées fpl contact details
copain m (male) friend
mon petit copain my boyfriend
copine f (female) friend
ma petite copine my girlfriend
corps m body
correct m, correcte f right, correct
correspond: **ça correspond à** it goes with, matches
correspondant m, **correspondante** f pen-pal
corrige correct
côte f coast
sur la côte on the coast
coucou! hi!
couleur f colour
coupé cut
on a coupé l'électricité the electricity was cut off
couple m couple
cours m lesson
courses: **faire les courses** to do the food shopping
cousin m, **cousine** f cousin
coûter to cost
coûter cher to be expensive
craqué cracked
il a craqué it cracked
crayon m pencil
crème f cream
cri m scream
cricket m cricket
cruel m, cruelle f cruel
cuisine f kitchen
faire la cuisine to do the cooking
curry m curry
cyclisme m cycling

D

d'accord OK
d'abord first of all, to begin with
danger m danger
en danger endangered
dangereux m, dangereuse f dangerous
dans in
dans le nord in the north
dans le bon ordre in the right order
danser to dance
on a dansé we danced
date f date
de 1 of: la capitale de la France the capital of France
2 de la f some, any
3 from: de 10h à 18h from 10 am to 6 pm
de rien don't mention it
début m beginning
décider (de) to decide (to)
décembre December
en décembre in December
déclaré declared
il, elle a déclaré he, she declared
décrire to describe
décris describe
définition f definition

déjeuner to have lunch
déjeuner m lunch
délicieux m, délicieuse f delicious
demain tomorrow
demie f half
il est six heures et demie it's half-past six
demi-frère m half-brother, step-brother
demi-sœur f half-sister, step-sister
demander to ask (for)
départ m departure
dépend: **ça dépend** it depends
depuis for, since
depuis longtemps? for how long?
depuis quatre jours for four days
dernier m, dernière f last
l'année dernière last year
des some
tu as des frères et sœurs? do you have any brothers and sisters?
désastreux m, désastreuse f
description f description
détail m detail
détective m detective
détester to detest, hate
je déteste ça I hate that
deux two
devant in front of
devoirs mpl homework
je dois faire mes devoirs I have to do my homework
diagramme m diagram
dialogue f dialogue
dictionnaire m dictionary
différence f difference
différent m, différente f different
un peu différent a bit different
difficile m or f difficult
dimanche m Sunday, on Sunday
diminué diminished
a diminué has diminished
dîner to have one's evening meal
dîner m evening meal
discussion f discussion
discutent: ils discutent they discuss
discuter de to discuss
disparition f disappearance
disponibilité f availability
dispute f argument
distribué distributed
il, elle a distribué he, she distributed
distribuer to distribue
dit 1 says: il, elle dit he, she says (from dire)
2 said: il, elle a dit he, she said
divorcent: ils divorcent they divorce
dix ten
dois: je dois I must (from devoir)
doit: il, elle doit he, she must, has to (from devoir)
doivent: ils doivent they have to (from devoir)
donner to give
donne les détails à ton/ta partenaire give your partner the details
dos m back
douze twelve
droit m, droite f right-hand
droite: à droite on the right
drogue: il se drogue he takes drugs
du m 1 some: du gâteau au chocolat some chocolate cake
2 from: du 02/05 au 30/09 from 2nd May to 30th September.
dû had to
j'ai dû I had to (past tense of devoir)
DVD m DVD

E

eau f water
eau minérale mineral water
échange m exchange
nous faisons un échange (avec) we're doing an exchange (with)
échos mpl gossip
les derniers échos the latest gossip
éclair m éclair
éclair au chocolat chocolate éclair
école f school
économiser to save
écossais m, écossaise f Scottish
Écosse f Scotland
écouté listened
j'ai écouté I listened (to)
écouter to listen (to)
écoute listen
j'écoute de la musique I listen to music
écouteurs mpl headphones
écrire to write
écris write
ça s'écrit comment? how do you spell it?
écris-moi bientôt write to me soon
écris les phrases dans le bon ordre write the sentences in the correct order
écrit wrote
j'ai écrit I wrote (past tense of écrire)
écrivez-moi write to me
électricité f electricity
électrique m or f electric
élevage m breeding, rearing
l'élevage en batterie battery farming
élève m or f pupil
elle she
elles they (females)
émission f (TV) programme:
1 de cuisine cookery
2 de sport sports
3 de musique music
en 1 in: en été in summer
en Afrique in, to Africa
en août in August
2 to: je suis allé en France I went to France
en bas downstairs
en bus by bus
en direct live
en français in French
en haut upstairs
endroit m place
enfant m or f child
enfin at last
énigme f puzzle, mystery
ennuyeux m, ennuyeuse f boring
énorme m or f enormous
enquêter (sur) to investigate
ensemble together
ensuite then
entendu heard
j'ai entendu I heard
tu as entendu? did you hear?
enthousiaste m or f enthusiastic
entre between
entré went into, entered
je suis entré(e) dans I went into
envers m the other side
à l'envers upside down
environ around, about
envoyé sent
j'ai envoyé I sent
envoyer to send
épisode f episode
épousé married
il, elle a épousé he, she married
équipe f team
erreur f mistake

Glossaire français–anglais

es: **tu es** *you are*
 tu es anglais(e)? *are you English?*
espagnol *m*, **espagnole** *f* *Spanish*
espoir *m hope*
 il y a de l'espoir *there is hope*
est 1 *is*: c'est *it is*
 2 *east*: dans l'est de la France *in the east of France*
est-ce que = *expression to begin a question*
 est-ce qu'il y a...? *is there...?*
estimer *to estimate*
estomac *m stomach*
et *and*
 et toi? *what about you?*
établir *to install*
étage *m floor*
 au premier étage *on the first floor*
étaient: ils, elles étaient *were*
était: il, elle était *he, she was*
 c'était *it was*
États-Unis *mpl United States*
été 1 *was (past tense of être)*:
 j'ai été *I was*
 2 *summer*: en été *in summer*
êtes: **vous êtes** *you are (from être)*
être *to be*
eu *had*
 j'ai eu *I had (past tense of avoir)*
 elle a eu *she had*
euro *m euro (French currency)*
Europe *f Europe*
européen *m*, **européenne** *f European*
excellent *m*, **excellente** *f excellent*
exception *f exception*
exceptionnel *m*, **exceptionnelle** *f exceptional*
exclusion *f exclusion, expulsion*
 une semaine d'exclusion *a week's suspension*
excursion *f excursion, trip*
exemple *m example*
 par exemple *for example*
exercice *f exercise*
expliquer *to explain*
expression *f expression*
extérieur: à l'extérieur *out of doors*
extraordinaire *m or f extraordinary*
extrait *m extract*
extraverti *m*, **extravertie** *f extrovert*

F

facile *m or f easy*
faim: j'ai faim *I'm hungry*
 tu as faim? *are you hungry?*
faire 1 *to do, make*:
 faire du sport *to do sport*
 faire la cuisine *to do the cooking*
 faire un échange *to do an exchange*
 2 *to go*:
 faire de la voile *to go sailing*
 faire du cheval *to go horseriding*
 faire du cyclisme *to go cycling*
 faire du go-karting *to go go-karting*
 faire du vélo *to go cycling*
 faire les magasins *to go round the shops*
fais *do (from faire)*
 je fais du shopping *I go shopping*
 je fais de la natation *I go swimming*
 je fais du vélo *I go cycling*
 je fais du canoë *I go canoeing*
 je fais de l'exercice *I take exercise*
 je fais mes devoirs *I do my homework*
faisait *was (doing)*
 il faisait mauvais *the weather was bad*

fait 1 *does (from faire)*: il, elle fait *he, she does*
 il fait la connaissance de *he makes the acquaintance of*
 2 *done (past tense of faire)*: j'ai fait *I did*
 il, elle a fait *he, she did*
 j'ai fait de la natation *I went swimming*
faites *do*
 vous faites *you (pl) do*
famille *f family*
fan *m fan*
fantastique *m or f fantastic*
fast-food *m fast food*
fatigue *f tiredness*
fauteuil *m armchair*
faux *m*, **fausse** *f false*
 vrai ou faux? *true or false?*
féminin *m*, **féminine** *f feminine*
femme *f woman*
fenêtre *f window*
ferme *f farm*
fermer *to close*
festival *m festival*
fête *f feast, festival*
 fête de la musique *music festival*
feuille *f (de papier) sheet (of paper)*
février *February*
fille *f girl*
film *m film*
 film policier *detective film*
fils *m son*
fin *f end*
finalement *finally*
fini *finished*
 j'ai fini *I've finished, I finished*
finir *to finish*
finit *finishes (from finir)*
 il, elle finit *he, she finishes (from finir)*
foot, football *m football*
 j'ai joué au foot *I played football*
footballeur *m footballer*
formulaire *f form*
fraise *f strawberry*
français *m*, **française** *f French*
France *f France*
frère *m brother*
frites *fpl chips*
froid *m*, **froide** *f cold*
 il fait froid *the weather is cold*
fromage *m cheese*
fruits *mpl fruit*
 elle mange beaucoup de fruits *she eats a lot of fruit*
fumer *to smoke*
fumier *m manure*
 l'odeur de fumier *the smell of manure*
futur *m future (tense)*
 au futur *in the future (tense)*

G

gagné *won*
 ils, elles ont gagné *they won*
gagner *to win*
gangsta rap *m gangsta rap*
garçon *m boy*
gâteau *m cake*
 gâteau au chocolat *chocolate cake*
gauche *f left*
 à gauche *on the left*
gendarme *m policeman*
généralement *generally*
génial *m*, **géniale** *f great*
 c'était génial! *it was great!*
genou *m knee*
gens *mpl people*
géographie *f geography*
glace *f ice cream*
glossaire *m glossary*

gorge *f throat*
 j'ai mal à la gorge *I have a sore throat*
gorille *m gorilla*
graffitis *mpl graffiti*
grammaire *f grammar*
gramme *m gram*
grand *m*, **grande** *f big*
 les grandes villes *big towns, cities*
 les grandes vacances *the summer holidays*
Grande-Bretagne *f Great Britain*
grand-mère *f grandmother*
grand-père *m grandfather*
grands-parents *mpl grandparents*
grille *f grid*
gros mots *mpl bad language*
grotte *f cave*
groupe *m group*
 mon groupe préféré *my favourite group*
 en groupes *in groups*
guide *m* 1 *(tour) guide* 2 *TV guide*
gymnase *m gymnasium*

H

habitant *m*, **habitante** *f inhabitant*
habité *lived*
 j'ai habité *I lived*
habiter *to live*
 j'habite à *I live in Biarritz*
 j'habite dans le sud-ouest *I live in the south west*
hamburger *m hamburger*
handball *m handball*
haut *m*, **haute** *f high*
 plus haut *higher*
hélicoptère *m helicopter*
 par hélicoptère *by helicopter*
héroïne *f heroin*
héros *m hero*
 héros mythiques *mythical heroes*
heure *f* 1 *hour* 2 *time*
 à quelle heure? *at what time?*
 à huit heures *at eight o'clock*
heureux *m*, **heureuse** *f happy*
hier *yesterday*
hilarant *m*, **hilarante** *f hilarious*
histoire *f* 1 *story* 2 *history*
historique *m or f historic*
hiver *m winter*
 en hiver *in winter*
hollandais *m*, **hollandaise** *f Dutch*
homme *m man*
hôpital *m (pl hôpitaux) hospital*
horrible *m or f horrible*
hot-dog *m hot-dog*
hourrah! *hurrah!*
huit *eight*
hyper: hyper beau *really lovely*

I

ici *here*
idée *f idea*
 bonne idée! *good idea!*
identifier *to identify, pick out*
idiot *m*, **idiote** *f crazy*
 c'est idiot! *it's crazy!*
il 1 *he*: il a *he has*
 il a été *he was*
 il avait marché sur *he had stood on*
 il est *he is*
 il fait *he does*
 il va passer *he is going to spend (time)*
 il se drogue *he takes drugs*
 2 *it*: il s'est retourné *it overturned*
 il faisait mauvais *the weather was bad*
 il fait beau *the weather is fine*
 il fait froid *the weather is cold*
 il fait mauvais *the weather is bad*

il y a *there is, are*
  il n'y a pas *there isn't*
  il n y a personne *there is no-one*
  il n'y a pas beaucoup de *there aren't many*
  il y a beaucoup de *there are lots of*
  il y a eu un cri terrible *there was a loud scream*
  il y avait *there was*
illusion d'optique *f optical illusion*
imaginer *to imagine*
immédiatement *immediately*
impatient *m*, **impatiente** *f impatient*
impertinent *m*, **impertinente** *f cheeky*
important *m*, **importante** *f importante*
  il n'y a personne d'important *there's nobody important*
impossible *m or f impossible*
impression *f impression*
impressionniste *m or f impressionist (painter)*
incendie *m fire*
industriel *m*, **industrielle** *f industrial*
informations *fpl information*
informatique *m technology*
inquiet *m*, **inquiète** *f worried*
inspecteur *m inspector*
installations électriques *fpl electrical installations*
instrument de musique *m musical instrument*
intelligent *m*, **intelligente** *f intelligent*
intéressant *m*, **intéressant** *f interesting*
international *m*, **internationale** *f international*
Internet *m internet*
  sur Internet *on the internet*
intrus: trouve l'intrus *find the odd one out*
inventé *invented*
  ils ont inventé *they invented*
inventer *to invent*
invisible *m or f invisible*
inviter *to invite*
irlandais *m*, **irlandaise** *f Irish*
Irlande du Nord *f Northern Ireland*
Italie *f Italy*
italien *m*, **italienne** *f Italian*

J

j' *I*
  j'ai *I have*
  j'ai 14 ans *I'm 14 years old*
  j'ai fait an tour sur *I went on (funfair ride)*
  j'ai mal à la tête *I have a headache*
  j'ai mal à l'estomac *I have stomach ache*
  j'ai mal au dos *my back aches*
  j'ai téléphoné (à) *I phoned*
  j'ai vomi *I was sick, vomited*
  j'aime *I like*
  j'écoute de la musique *I listen to music*
jamais *never*
  ne… jamais *never*
  je ne fume jamais *I never smoke*
jambon *m ham*
janvier *January*
  en Janvier *in January*
Japon *m Japan*
jardin *m garden*
jaune *m or f yellow*
je *I*
  je m'appelle *my name is*
  je n'ai pas de sœur *I don't have any sisters*
  je n'aime pas… *I don't like…*
  je ne fais jamais ça *I never do that*
  je peux vous aider *can I help you?*
  je veux bien *yes please*
jeu *m (pl jeux) TV quiz show*
  jeux vidéo *computer games*
  les Jeux olympiques *the Olympic Games*
jeudi *m Thursday, on Thursday*

jogging: *il fait du jogging*
joué *played*
  j'ai joué *I played*
jouer *to play*
  je joue au badminton *I play badminton*
  je joue au basket *I play basketball*
  je joue au football *I play football*
  je joue au ping-pong *I play table tennis*
  je joue aux cartes *I play cards*
  je joue sur Internet *I play on the internet*
jour *m day*
  tous les jours *every day*
journal *m (pl journaux) newspaper*
juillet *July*
  en juillet *in July*
juin *June*
jumeau *m*, **jumelle** *f twin*
jury *m jury*
jus *m juice*
  jus d'orange *orange juice*
  jus de fruits *fruit juice*

K

kangourou *m kangaroo*
karting *m go-kart*
  faire du karting *to go go-karting*
kayak *m kayak*
  faire du kayak *to go kayaking*
kilo *m kilogram*
kilomètre *m kilometre*
kung-fu *m kung fu*
  je fais du kung-fu *I do kung fu*

L

la *f 1 the 2 her, it*
là *there*
  oh là là *oh dear!*
là-bas *down there*
lait *m milk*
langue *f language*
le *1 m the 2 him, it 3 on, at:* le 30 mars *on the 30th March*
  le week-end *at the weekend*
légendaire *m or f legendary*
légumes *mpl vegetables*
les *pl the*
lettre *f letter*
lève: lève la main *put your hand up*
liberté *f liberty*
  en liberté *in the wild*
lieux: lieux de vacances *mpl holiday resorts*
limonade *f lemonade*
lion *m lion*
lire *to read*
  j'aime lire *I like reading*
lis: *1 je lis I read (from lire)*
  2 lis read
lisez *read*
liste *f list*
livre *m book*
logique *m or f logic*
loger *to stay*
  il va loger *he's going to stay*
loin *far*
  c'est loin? *is it far?*
Londres *London*
long *m*, **longue** *f long*
longtemps *long time*
  depuis longtemps *for a long time*
look *m look*
louer *to hire*
lu *read*
  j'ai lu *I read (past tense of lire)*
lui *him, to him*
lundi *Monday, on Monday*
  lundi dernier *last Monday*

Luxembourg *m Luxemburg*
lycée *m school*

M

ma *f my*
magasin *m (pl magasins) shop*
mai *May*
  en mai *in May*
main *f hand*
  lève la main *put your hand up*
maintenant *now*
maire *m mayor*
mais *but*
  mais non! *of course not!*
maison *f house*
  à la maison *at home*
  je rentre à la maison *I go home*
maître *m master*
mangé *ate*
  j'ai mangé une pizza *I ate a pizza*
  on a mangé *we ate*
manger *to eat*
mangez *eat*
marche *f walk, walking*
  je fais de la marche *I go walking*
marché *m market*
  on est allé au marché *we went to the market*
mardi *Tuesday, on Tuesday*
mariage *m marriage*
marié *m*, **mariée** *f married*
  il s'est marié avec *he got married to*
marin *m*, **marine** *f marine*
  la Marine nationale *navy*
marque *f label, brand*
mars *March*
  en mars *in March*
masculin *m masculine*
mât *m mast*
match *m match*
  match de foot *football*
maths *fpl maths*
  fais les maths *do the sums*
matin *m morning*
  le matin *in the morning*
  le samedi matin *on Saturday mornings*
mauvais *m*, **mauvaise** *f bad*
  il fait mauvais *the weather is bad*
médias *mpl media*
meilleur *m*, **meilleure** *f better, best*
mémoire *f memory*
  de mémoire *from memory*
menthe *f mint*
mentionné *m*, **mentionnée** *f mentioned*
mentionner *to mention*
mer *f sea*
  on est allé à la mer *we went to the seaside*
merci *thank you*
  merci pour tout *thank you for everything*
mercredi *Wednesday, on Wednesday*
mère *f mother*
mes *pl my*
métro *m underground*
miam-miam! *yum-yum!*
midi *m midday*
  à midi *at midday*
mille *1000*
milliard *m billion*
moderne *m or f modern*
moi *me*
  moi aussi *me too*
  moi, non *I don't, not me*
moins *less*
  à huit heures moins le quart *at a quarter to eight*
  à onze heures moins vingt *at twenty to eleven*
moment *m moment*

Glossaire français–anglais

mois *m* *month*
  le mois prochain *next month*
mon *m* *my*
monde *m* *world*
monsieur *m* 1 *Mr* 2 *Sir*
monstre *m* *monster*
montagne *f* *mountain*
mot *m* *word*
musée *m* *museum*
musicien *m*, **musicienne** *f* *musical*
musique *f* *music*
  musique classique *classical music*

N

n'aime: je n'aime pas *I don't like*
natation *f* *swimming*
  je fais de la natation *I go swimming*
national *m*, **nationale** *f* *national*
nationalité *f* *nationality*
nature *f* *nature*
ne… pas *(expresses a negative)*
  il n'était pas là *he wasn't there*
négatif *m*, **negative** *f* *negative*
neige *f* *snow*
  il neige *it's snowing*
neuf *nine*
noir *m*, **noire** *f* *black*
noisette *f* *hazelnut*
nom *m* *name*
nombre (de) *m* *number (of)*
non *no*
  non, merci *no thanks*
nord *m* *north*
normalement *normally*
nos *pl* *our*
noter *to note down*
notre *our*
nourriture *f* *food*
nous *we*
  nous avons *we have*
nouveau *m*, **nouvelle** *f* *new*
nuit *f* *night*
  la nuit la plus chaude de l'année *the hottest night of the year*
nul *m*, **nulle** *f* *bad, rubbish, awful*
numéro *m* *number*
  numéro de portable *mobile number*

O

octobre *October*
  en Octobre *in October*
odeur *m* *smell*
  l'odeur de fumier *the smell of manure*
offrir *to offer*
  on offre quoi? *what's on offer?*
oh là là! *oh dear!*
on *one, we*
  on a fait un tour sur *we went for a ride on*
  on a fait une excursion *we went on a trip*
  on va *we go*
  on va faire de la natation *we're going to go swimming*
oncle *m* *uncle*
ont: ils, elles ont *they have (from avoir)*
  ils ont inventé *they invented*
onze *eleven*
opéra *m* *opera*
opinion *f* *opinion*
option *f* *option, alternative*
  choisis la bonne option *choose the right option*
orange *orange (colour)*
orange *f* *orange (fruit)*
  un jus d'orange *orange juice*
orchestre *m* *orchestra*

ordinaire *m or f* *ordinary*
ordinateur *m* *computer*
ordre *m* *order*
  l'ordre chronologique *chronological order*
  dans le bon ordre *in the right order*
organisé *organised*
  il, elle a organisé *he, she organised*
original *m*, **originale** *f* *original*
os *m* *bone*
ou *or*
où *where*
  où habites-tu? *where do you live?*
ouest *m* *west*
oui *yes*
ours *m* *bear*
  ours polaire *polar bear*
ouvert *m*, **ouverte** *f* *open*

P

page: à la page 50 *on page 50*
pain *m* *bread*
paire *f* *pair*
  trouve les paires *find the matching pairs*
paniqué *panicked*
  je n'ai pas paniqué *I didn't panic*
pantalon *m* *trousers*
paparazzi *mpl* *paparazzi (pestering journalists & photographers)*
papier peint *m* *wallpaper*
paquet *m* *packet*
  paquet de chips *packet of crisps*
par *by, per*
  par an *per year*
  par exemple *for example*
paradis *m* *paradise*
parc *m* *park*
  parc d'attractions *theme park*
parce que *because*
pardon *excuse me*
parents *mpl* *parents*
paresseux *m*, **paresseuse** *f* *lazy*
parfois *sometimes*
parfum *m* *flavour*
parler *to speak*
partenaire *m or f* *partner*
  un collège partenaire *partner school*
partir *to leave*
  à partir de 14h *from 2pm onwards*
pas *not*
  pas beaucoup *not much*
  pas de problème *no problem*
  je n'aime pas *I don't like*
passage de train *m* *level crossing*
passant: en passant par *via*
passé maître *m* *past master*
passé *spent (time)*
  j'ai passé *I spent*
  j'ai passé un week-end super *I had a great weekend*
passer *to spend (time)*
  passer la nuit *to spend the night*
  il va passer *he's going to spend*
passe-temps *m* *pastime, hobby*
pâtes *fpl* *pasta*
patinoire *f* *skating rink*
pâtisserie *f* *cake shop*
patron *m*, **patronne** *f* *boss*
pause *f* *pause*
pauvre *m or f* *poor*
pays *m* **de Galles** *Wales*
pêcheur *m* *fisherman*
peintre *m* *painter*
peinture *f* *painting*
pendant *during, for*
pénible *hard, tough*
  c'est pénible *it's a pain*

perdu *lost*
  j'ai perdu *I lost (past tense of perdre)*
père *m* *father*
période *f* *period, time*
  une période difficile *a difficult time*
personnage *m* *character*
personne *f* 1 *person*
  2 ne… personne *nobody*
  il n'y a personne *there is no-one*
personnellement *personally*
persuadé *convinced, persuaded*
  je suis persuadé que *I'm convinced that*
petit *m*, **petite** *f* *small*
peu *a little*
  peu avant *just before*
peut: on peut *you can (from pouvoir)*
peut-être *perhaps, maybe*
peux: je ne peux pas *I can't (from pouvoir)*
  je peux avoir… ? *can I have… ?*
  je peux vous aider *can I help you?*
pharmacie *f* *chemist's*
phrase *f* *sentence*
piano *m* *piano*
pièce de théâtre *f* *play*
pied *m* *foot*
  j'ai mal aux pieds *my feet hurt*
  à pied *on foot*
ping-pong *m* *table tennis*
  je joue au ping-pong *I play table tennis*
pique-nique *m* *picnic*
pique-niquer *to have a picnic*
  nous avons pique-niqué *we had a picnic*
piscine *f* *swimming pool*
pizza *f* *pizza*
placer *to place, position*
plage *f* *beach*
plaît: s'il te/vous plaît *please*
pleut: il pleut *it's raining*
pluriel *m* *plural*
plus *more*
  plus tard *later*
  en plus *what's more*
  plus haut *higher*
  plus de *more than*
point *m* *dot (in e-mail address)*
poisson *m* *fish*
  poisson d'avril *April Fool*
polaire *m or f* *polar*
  ours polaire *polar bear*
pôle *m* *pole*
  le pôle nord/sud *north/south pole*
politique *f* *politics*
pollution *f* *pollution*
pomme *f* *apple*
pommes de terre *fpl* *potatoes*
pompiers *mpl* *firefighters*
populaire *m or f* *popular*
portable *m* *mobile phone*
porte *f* *door*
porte-monnaie *m* *purse*
poser (une question) *to ask (a question)*
  pose trois questions *ask 3 questions*
positif *m*, **positive** *f* *positive*
position *f* *position*
possibilité *f* *possibility*
possible *m or f* *possible*
postale: carte postale *f* *postcard*
poumons *mpl* *lungs*
pour *for*
  pour cent *per cent*
  pour faire *in order to make*
  pour toi *for you*
pourcentage *m* *percentage*
pourquoi? *why?*
pouvez: vous pouvez *you can (from pouvoir)*
  pouvez-vous répéter? *can you repeat (that)?*
préféré *m*, **préférée** *f* *favourite*
  mon groupe préféré *my favourite group*

préférer *to prefer*
  je préfère *I prefer*
  tu préfères… ? *do you prefer… ?*
premier *m*, **première** *f* *first*
  le premier mai *the first of May*
prend: on prend… ? *shall we take some… ?*
prends: je prends *I take*
prénom *m* *first name*
préparé *m*, **préparée** *f* *prepared*
  j'ai préparé *I prepared*
préparer *to prepare*
près (de) *near*
  près d'ici *near here*
  près de Biarritz *near Biarritz*
  il y a… près d'ici? *is there… near here?*
présent *m* *present (tense)*
présentation *f* *presentation*
présenter *to present*
  se présenter *to introduce yourself*
préserver *to protect (animals)*
pris *took*
  j'ai pris *I took (past tense of prendre)*
  ils ont pris le train *they took the train*
prix *m* 1 *price* 2 *prize*
probablement *probably*
problème *m* *problem*
  pas de problème *no problem*
prochain *m*, **prochaine** *f* *next*
prof *m or f* *teacher*
profession *f* *profession*
prononcer *to pronounce*
prononciation *f* *pronunciation*
public *m* *public*
publicités *fpl* *adverts*
puis *then*
Pyrénées *fpl* *the Pyrenees (mountains)*

Q

qu'est-ce que? *what?*
  qu'est-ce que tu aimes? *what do you like?*
qualité *f* *quality*
quand *when*
  c'est quand, ton anniversaire? *when's your birthday?*
quarante *forty*
quart *m* *quarter*
  onze heures moins le quart *a quarter to eleven*
quatorze *fourteen*
quatre *four*
quatre-vingts *eighty*
quatre-vingt-dix *ninety*
quatrième *fourth*
quel *m*, **quelle** *f* *what, which*
  quel âge as-tu? *how old are you?*
  à quelle heure? *at what time*
  c'est quelle photo? *which photo is it?*
quel temps fait-il? *what's the weather like?*
quelque *some*
  quelque chose à manger *something to eat*
question *f* *question*
qui 1 *who:* c'est qui? *who is it?*
  qui s'appelle *who is called*
  2 *which*
quinze *fifteen*
quitté *left*
  j'ai quitté *I left*
quitter *to leave*
quoi *what*
  c'est quoi ton groupe préféré? *what's your favourite group?*
  tu as fait quoi le week-end dernier? *what did you do last weekend?*
  c'est quoi, ton adresse? *what's your address?*

R

radio *f* *radio*
  à la radio *on the radio*
range-CD *mpl* *CD racks*
rapides *mpl* *rapids*
rappeur *m* *rapper*
ravagé *ravaged*
  un incendie a ravagé *a fire ravaged*
réalise *produced*
  il, elle a réalisé *he, she produced (a film)*
réception *f* *reception*
recherche *f* *search*
  à la recherche de… *the search for…*
reçoit *receives*
  il, elle reçoit *he, she receives*
recopie *copy*
réécoute *listen again*
regarder *to watch*
  je regarde des vidéos *I watch videos*
  tu regardes des séries? *do you watch soaps?*
regardé *watched*
  j'ai regardé *I watched*
regardez *look*
région *f* *area*
regrette: je regrette *I'm sorry*
relie les paires *link up the pairs*
relis *re-read*
rencontré *met*
  j'ai rencontré *I met*
rencontrer *to meet*
rendre: rendre visite à *to pay a visit*
renvoyé *sacked*
  vous êtes renvoyé *you're sacked*
répète *repeat*
répéter *to repeat*
répondre *to answer*
réponds *answer*
réponse *f* *answer*
reportage *m* *report*
république *m* *republic*
  République Tchèque *Czech Republic*
ressembler à *to look like*
restaurant *m* *restaurant*
rester *to stay*
retourné *overturned*
  il s'est retourné *it overturned*
retraite *f* *retirement*
retrouvé *found*
  j'ai retrouvé mes copains *I met up with my friends*
révélation *f* *revelation*
revenir *to come back*
revient: il, elle revient *he, she comes back*
révolte *f* *revolt*
riche *m or f* *rich*
ridicule *m or f* *ridiculous*
rien *nothing*
  de rien *don't mention it*
rigoles: tu rigoles! *you're joking!*
rigolo: ce n'est pas rigolo *it's no joke*
ri *laughed*
  on a ri *we laughed (past tense of rire)*
rire *to laugh*
rivière *f* *river*
rôle: joue le rôle de *play the part of*
roller coaster *m* *rollercoaster*
Romains *mpl* *Romans*
rompu *broke*
  il, elle a rompu avec *he, she broke up with*
roue *m* *wheel*
  la grande roue *the big wheel (at funfair)*
rouge *m or f* *red*
  en rouge *in red*
route *f* *way*
  en route pour *on the way to*

Royaume-Uni *m* *United Kingdom*
rue *f* *street*
rugby *m* *rugby*
  je joue au rugby *I play rugby*
Russie *f* *Russia*

S

s'il te plaît *please (to friend)*
s'il vous plaît *please (to adult)*
sa *f* *his, her*
safari *m* *safari*
  j'ai fait un safari *I went on safari*
sais *know*
  je sais *I know (from savoir)*
  je ne sais pas *I don't know*
salade *f* *salad*
  salade de fruits tropicaux *tropical fruit salad*
salon *m* *living room*
salut! *hi! hello!*
samedi *Saturday, on Saturday*
  à samedi! *see you on Saturday!*
sandwich *m* *sandwich*
  un sandwich au fromage *a cheese sandwich*
sang *m* *blood*
sans *without*
s'appellent: ils s'appellent *they are called*
satellite *m* *satellite (TV)*
savais: je ne savais pas *I couldn't*
secret *m* *secret*
  en secret *in secret*
Scandinavie *f* *Scandinavia*
scolaire *m or f* *school*
  voyage scolaire *school trip*
sépare: ils se séparent *they separate*
seize *sixteen*
séjour *m* *stay*
  un bon séjour *a good trip*
sel *m* *salt*
sélection *f* *selection*
sélectionné(e) *chosen*
sélectionner *to select*
semaine *f* *week*
  une semaine d'exclusion *a week's suspension*
  la semaine prochaine *next week*
  pendant la semaine *during the week*
sept *seven*
série *f* *series, soap (TV)*
ses *pl* *his, her*
shopping *m* *shopping*
  je fais du shopping *I go shopping*
show *m* *TV show*
si *if*
  s'il vous plaît *please*
  si nécessaire *if necessary*
similaire *m or f* *similar*
site *m* *site*
  le site web *website*
situation *f* *situation*
situé: est situé *is situated*
six *six*
ski *m* *skiing*
  je fais du ski *I go skiing*
sœur *f* *sister*
  sœur jumelle *a twin sister*
soif: j'ai soif *I'm thirsty*
  tu as soif? *are you thirsty?*
soir *m* *evening*
  le soir *in the evening*
  lundi soir *on Monday evening*
soirée *f* *party*
soixante *sixty*
soixante-dix *seventy*
soixante-quinze *seventy five*
soleil *m* *sun*
solliciter *to approach, to appeal to*
solo: en solo *solo (album)*

Glossaire français–anglais

sommaire *m* summary
sommes: nous sommes we are
son *m* his
sont: ils, elles sont they are (from être)
sors go out
  je sors avec mes copains *I go out with my friends*
sort: il, elle sort he, she goes out (from sortir)
sortir to go out
soudain suddenly
souligné *m*, **soulignée** *f* underlined
souhaiter to wish
  je te souhaite *I wish you*
soupe *f* soup
souris *f* mouse
souri smiled
  il m'a souri *he smiled at me*
sourire to smile
sous under
souvenir *m* souvenir
souvent often
spécial *m* (*pl* spéciaux), **spéciale** *f* special
spectacle *m* show
sportif *m*, **sportive** *f* sporty
stade *m* stadium
stalactite *f* stalactite
stalagmite *f* stalagmite
star *f* (film, music) star
station *f* resort
  station de vacances *holiday resort*
stratégies *fpl* strategies, tips
strict *m*, **stricte** *f* strict
stupide *m or f* stupid
style de vie *m* lifestyle
succès *m* success
sucre *m* sugar
sud *m* south
sud-ouest *m* southwest
suis am
  je suis *I am (from être)*
  je suis allé(e) en Australie *I went to Australia*
  je suis contre la chasse *I'm against hunting*
  je suis enfant unique *I'm an only child*
Suisse *f* Switzerland
suisse *m or f* Swiss
super great, super
  c'était super *it was great*
supermarché *m* supermarket
supporter to support
supposer: je suppose I suppose
sur 1 on: sur Internet *on the internet*
  2 about: recherches sur la musique *research about music*
sûr *m*, **sûre** *f* sure
  bien sûr *of course*
surf: faire du surf to go surfing
surfer to surf
surprise *f* surprise
surtout especially
suspect *m* suspect
symbole *m* symbol
sympa *m or f* nice

T

ta *f* your
tabac *m* tobacconist's, newsagent
table *f* table
  à table *at the table*
talent *m* talent
  elle a beaucoup de talent *she is very talented*
talk-shows *mpl* talk shows
tamponneuses: autos tamponneuses bumper cars
tant: en tant que as

tard late
  plus tard *later*
tchatché chatted
  j'ai tchatché sur Internet *I chatted on the Internet*
tchatcher to chat (online)
tchèque *m or f* Czech
  la République Tchèque *Czech Republic*
technologie *f* technology
télé *f* TV
  à la télé *on TV*
téléphoner à to phone somebody
télé-réalité *f* reality TV
temps *m* weather
  quel temps fait-il? *what's the weather like?*
tennis *m* tennis
  je joue au tennis *I play tennis*
tennis de table *m* table tennis
terrifiant *m*, **terrifiante** *f* terrifying
tes *pl* your
tête *f* head
texte *m* text
théâtre *m* theatre
thé *m* tea
  thé au lait *tea with milk*
thème *m* theme
tigre *m* tiger
timide *m or f* shy
toi you
  et toi? *what about you?*
  chez toi *at your house*
toilettes *fpl* toilet
ton *m* your
top: c'est vraiment top! *it's really great!*
toujours always
tour *m* 1 tour, trip
  2 tower: la tour Eiffel *Eiffel Tower*
  3 turn: à ton tour *your turn*
touriste *m or f* tourist
tourner to turn
tournoi *m* tournament
tous *mpl* all, every
  tous les jours *every day*
tout *m*, **toute** *f* all
  c'est tout *that's all*
  toutes les 30 minutes *every 30 minutes*
train *m* train
  en train *by train*
trait *m* trait
  trait de caractère *personality trait*
transporté transported
  il a été transporté *he was transported*
travailler to work
treize thirteen
trente thirty
très very
trois three
troisième *m or f* third
trop (de) too much, too many
trouvé found
  il a été trouvé *it was found*
trouver to find
  trouve les paires *find the matching pairs*
tu you
  tu as des frères et sœurs? *have you any brothers and sisters?*
  tu as fait quoi le week-end? *what did you do at the weekend?*
  tu as vu? *did you see?*
  tu es pour ou contre? *are you for or against?*
type *m* sort, type

U

un one
un *m*, **une** *f* a
unique *m or f* only
  je suis enfant unique *I'm an only child*

V

va: il, elle va he, she goes (from aller)
  on va *we go*
vacances *fpl* holidays
  lieux de vacances *mpl* holiday destinations
vais: je vais faire du ski *I'm going skiing*
  je vais aux toilettes *I'm going to the toilet*
  je vais lui rendre visite *I'm going to pay him, her a visit*
  je vais aller passer une semaine *I'm going to spend a week*
vas: tu vas… ? do you go… ?
vélo *m* bike, bicycle
  je fais du vélo *I go cycling*
  faire du vélo *to go cycling*
vendredi Friday, on Friday
venir to come
verbe *m* verb
vérifier to check
vers around
  vers 10 heures *around 10 o'clock*
vert *m*, **verte** *f* green
vêtements *mpl* clothes
  vêtements de marque *designer clothes*
vétérinaire *m or f* vet
  ma mère est vétérinaire *my mother is a vet*
veux: tu veux… ? do you want… ? (from vouloir)
  je veux bien *yes please*
viande *f* meat
victime *f* victim
vie *f* life
vierges: des CD vierges blank CDs
village *m* village
ville *f* town
  en ville *in town*
vin *m* wine
vingt twenty
violence *f* violence
  il y a trop de violence *there is too much violence*
violent *m*, **violente** *f* violent
violon *m* violin
visite *f* visit
  une visite guidée *guided tour*
visité visited
  on a visité *we visited*
  nous avons visité *we visited*
visiteur *m* visitor
vivre to live
voici here is
voilà there you are
voile *f* sailing
  faire de la voile *to go sailing*
voir to see
voiture *f* car
  en voiture *by car*
volley *m* volleyball
  on a joué au volley *we played volleyball*
vomi vomited, was sick
  j'ai vomi *I vomited, was sick*
vont: ils vont they go (from aller)
vote *m* vote
votre your
voudrais would like
  je voudrais *I'd like*

vous *you* (1 *to adult* 2 *to more than one person*)
   pouvez-vous répéter? *could you repeat?*
   vous faites quoi le week-end? *what do you do at the weekend?*
voyage m *trip*
   bon voyage! *have a good trip!*
   voyage scolaire *school trip*
   c'est mon premier voyage scolaire *it's my first school trip*

voyager *to travel*
   voyager avec ma famille *to travel with my family*
vrai f, **vraie** m *true*
   c'est vrai *it's true*
   ce n'est pas vrai *it's not true*
vraiment *really, truly*
VTT: faire du VTT *to go mountain-biking*
vu: j'ai vu *I saw (from avoir)*

W
week-end m *weekend*

Z
zoo f *zoo*

Glossaire anglais–français

A
a, an **un** m, **une** f
advert **la publicité** f
after **après**
afternoon **l'après-midi** m
   in the afternoon **l'après-midi**
against **contre**
   I'm against… **je suis contre…**
airport **l'aéroport** m
all: is that all? **c'est tout?**
also **aussi**
always **toujours**
am: I am **je suis** (see **être** p. 127)
and **et**
April **avril**
are (see **être**, p. 127)
   there are **il y a**
arrive: I arrive **j'arrive**
at: 1 at my friend's house **chez ma copine**, at my house **chez moi**
   2 at school **au collège**, at home **à la maison**
ate: I ate **j'ai mangé**
August **août**
aunt **la tante** f
autumn: in autumn **en automne**
awful: it's awful **c'est nul**

B
bad language **les gros mots** mpl
banana **la banane** f
bank **la banque** f
barbecue **le barbecue** m
basketball **le basket** m
   I play basketball **je joue au basket**
battle **la bataille** f
beach **la plage** f
because **parce que**
Belgium **la Belgique** f
best: the best **le meilleur** m, **la meilleure** f
between **entre**
big **grand** m, **grande** f
bike **le vélo** m
   by bike **à vélo**
birthday **l'anniversaire** m
black **noir** m, **noire** f
blue **bleu** m, **bleue** f
book **le livre** m
boring: it's boring **c'est barbant**
bottle (of) **la bouteille** f (de)
bowling alley **le bowling** m
bought: I bought **j'ai acheté**
boxing **la boxe** f
boy **le garçon** m
bridge **le pont** m
British **britannique** m or f
brother **le frère** m

brown **marron** m or f
bus **le bus** m
   by bus **en bus**
but **mais**
button **le bouton** m
by: 1 by car **en auto**
   2 by bike **à vélo**

C
café **le café** m
cake **le gâteau** m
camping: I go camping **je fais du camping**
campsite **le camping** m
can: can I… ? **je peux… ?**
car **l'auto** f, **la voiture** f
   by car **en auto**
cards: I play cards **je joue aux cartes**
castle **le château** m
cat **le chat** m
CD **le CD** m (pl *les CD*)
cells: nerve cells **les cellules nerveuses** fpl
centre: sports centre **le centre sportif** m
   shopping centre **le centre commercial**
   leisure centre **le centre de loisirs**
chat: we chat **on bavarde**
chatted: we chatted **on a bavardé**
cheese **le fromage** m
cheeky **impertinent** m, **impertinente** f
child **enfant** m or f
   I'm an only child **je suis enfant unique**
chips **les frites** fpl
chocolate **le chocolat** m
choir **la chorale** f
church **l'église** f
clothes **les vêtements** mpl
click **clique**
coach **le car** m
coffee **le café** m
   a white coffee **un grand crème**
cold: the weather is cold **il fait froid**
come: I come **je viens**
comfortable **confortable** m or f
computer **l'ordinateur** m
computer games **les jeux vidéo** mpl
cookery: cookery programme **l'émission de cuisine** f
cost: how much does it cost? **c'est combien?**
could: could you repeat? **pouvez-vous répéter?**
country **le pays** m
   in the country **à la campagne**
crisps **les chips** fpl
cup: World Cup **la Coupe du Monde** f

D
day **le jour** m
dear **cher** m, **chère** f
detective **le détective** m
dictionary **le dictionnaire** m
did: I did **j'ai fait**
difficult **difficile** m or f
do: I do **je fais** (see p. 128)
   I do my homework **je fais mes devoirs**
doesn't: it doesn't snow **il ne neige pas**
he doesn't play **il ne joue pas**
dog **le chien** m
don't: I don't like **je n'aime pas**
drink: I drink **je bois**
drank: I drank **j'ai bu**
drugs: he takes drugs **il se drogue**
during **pendant**

E
each **chaque**
easy **facile** m or f
eat: I eat **je mange**
eighty **quatre-vingts**
England **l'Angleterre** f
   in England **en Angleterre**
entertainments **les distractions** fpl
evening **le soir** m
   in the evening **le soir**
everybody **tout le monde**
exercise book **le cahier** m
extrovert **extraverti** m, **extravertie** f

F
family **la famille** f
famous **célèbre** m or f
fashionable **en mode**
father **le père** m
favourite **préféré** m, **préférée** f
February **février**
fifty **cinquante**
first **premier** m, **première** f
fish **le poisson** m
flavour: what flavour? **quel parfum?**
foggy: it's foggy **il fait du brouillard**
foot **le pied** m
   on foot **à pied**
football **le football** m
   I play football **je joue au football**
football stadium **le stade de football** m
for **pour**
   I'm for… **je suis pour…**
forty **quarante**
fountain **la fontaine** f
France **la France** f
   to France **en France**
French **français** m, **française** f

Glossaire anglais–français

Friday **vendredi**
friend **copain** m, **copine** f
front: in front of **devant**
fun: it's fun **c'est amusant**
  it was fun **c'était amusant**
funny **amusant** m, **amusante** f

G
game **le jeu** m (pl jeux)
  computer games **les jeux vidéo**
  (TV) game shows **les jeux**
gameboy **la console de jeux** f
gangsta rap **le gangsta rap** m
garden **le jardin** m
Germany **l'Allemagne** f
girl **la fille** f
give: I give **je donne**
go: I go **je vais** (see p. 128)
  I go cycling **je fais du vélo**
  I go sailing **je fais de la voile**
good-bye **au revoir**
good-looking **beau** m, **belle** f
grapes **le raisin** m
great **super**, **génial** m or f
green **vert** m, **verte** f
group **le groupe** m
gymnastics **la gymnastique** f
  I do gymnastics **je fais de la gymnastique**

H
had: I had **j'ai eu**
half: at half past six **à six heures et demie**
ham **le jambon** m
happy 1 **joyeux** m, **joyeuse** f happy New
  Year! *bonne année!*
  2 **heureux** m, **heureuse** f
hard **difficile** m or f
have **avoir** (see p. 127)
he **il**
hello **bonjour, salut**
here **ici**
hi **salut**
hire: I hire videos **je loue des vidéos**
hobby **le passe-temps** m
home 1 at home **à la maison**
  2 I come home **je rentre à la maison**
homework **les devoirs** mpl
honey **le miel** m
horse **le cheval** m (pl **chevaux**)
horse-riding **l'équitation** f
  I go horse-riding *je fais du cheval*
hot: the weather is hot **il fait chaud**
house **la maison** f
  at my house *chez moi*
how 1 **comment**
  2 how many? **combien?**, how much is it?
  c'est combien?
hundred **cent**
hungry: I'm hungry **j'ai faim**
hustle and bustle **le brouhaha** m

I
ice cream **la glace** f
  some ice cream *de la glace*
ice rink **la patinoire** f
in 1 **dans**
  2 in London **à Londres**
  3 'in' = in fashion **en mode**
interesting **intéressant** m, **intéressante** f
Ireland **l'Irlande** f
  in Ireland *en Irlande*
  in Northern Ireland *en Irlande du Nord*
is **est** (see verb **être** p. 127)
  it is *c'est*
  there is *il y a*
  it's **c'est**

J
January **janvier**
journey **le voyage** m
juice **le jus** m
  an orange juice *un jus d'orange*
  some juice *du jus*
July **juillet**
June **juin**

K
kitchen **la cuisine** f

L
lazy **paresseux** m, **paresseuse** f
last: last weekend **le week-end dernier**
lemon **le citron** m
  some lemon *du citron*
less **moins**
lesson **le cours** m
library **la bibliothèque** f
like 1 I like **j'aime**
  2 I'd like **je voudrais**
  3 like a lion **comme un lion**
  4 what is it like? **c'est comment?**
listen: I listen (to music) **j'écoute (de la
  musique)**
live: I live **j'habite**
  he lives *il habite*
London **Londres**
long **long** m, **longue** f
lost: I've lost **j'ai perdu**
lot: a lot (of) **beaucoup** (de)
loud **bruyant** m, **bruyante** f
love: I love **j'adore, j'aime** (beaucoup)
lunch: I have lunch **je déjeune**
  packed lunch *le repas froid*

M
manure **le fumier** m
map **la carte** f
March **mars**
market **le marché** m
marmalade **la marmelade d'oranges** f
married **marié** m, **mariée** f
May **mai**
me **moi**
meat **la viande** f
midday: at midday **à midi**
milk **le lait** m
mint **la menthe** f
Miss **Mademoiselle** f, (at school) **Madame** f
Monday **lundi**
more **plus**
morning **le matin** m
  in the morning *le matin*
mother **la mère** f
motorbike **la moto** f
mountain **la montagne** f
mouse **la souris** f
much: how much is it? **c'est combien?**
  I don't like cats much *je n'aime pas beaucoup
  les chats*
murderer **l'assassin** m
museum **le musée** m
music **la musique** f
musical **musicien** m, **musicienne** f
must: I must **je dois**
  I must do the washing-up *je dois faire la
  vaisselle*
my **mon** m, **ma** f, **mes** pl

N
nature **la nature** f
nature reserve **la réserve naturelle** f
near **près de**
next **prochain** m, **prochaine** f
  next week *la semaine prochaine*

never **jamais**
nice **sympa** m or f
  the weather is nice *il fait beau*
ninety **quatre-vingt-dix**
no **non**

O
of **de**
of course **bien sûr**
often **souvent**
OK **d'accord**
old **vieux** m, **vieille** f
  how old are you? *quel âge as-tu?*
opinion: in my opinion **à mon avis**
or **ou**
other **autre**

P
packed lunch **le repas froid** m
packet (of) **le paquet** m (de)
park **le parc** m
  theme park *le parc d'attractions*
party **la soirée** f
pear **la poire** f
pen 1 biro **le bic** m
  2 fountain pen *le stylo* m
pencil **le crayon** m
perhaps **peut-être**
person **la personne** f
pet **l'animal** m (pl **animaux**)
phone: I phone **je téléphone**
picnic **un pique-nique** m
play **jouer**
  I play tennis *je joue au tennis*
played: I played **j'ai joué**
please **s'il te plaît** (to friend), **s'il vous plaît**
  (to adult)
politics **la politique** f
pollution **la pollution** f
porridge: some porridge **du porridge**
post office **la poste** f
prefer: I prefer **je préfère**
  do you prefer? **tu préfères?**
present **le cadeau** m
programme: TV **une émission de télé** f
price **le prix** m
pupil **élève** m or f

Q
quite **assez**
  quite hard *assez difficile*

R
rabbit **le lapin** m
railway station **la gare** f
rain: it's raining **il pleut**
read: I read **je lis**
reality: TV **la télé-réalité** f
red **rouge** m or f
resort: holiday resorts **les lieux de vacances**
  mpl
rich **riche** m or f
ring **la bague** f
rock concert **le concert de rock** m
room **la chambre** f
rugby **le rugby** m
  I play rugby *je joue au rugby*

S
sailing **la voile** f
  I go sailing *je fais de la voile*
Saturday **samedi**
saw: I saw **j'ai vu**
say: how do you say "friend" in French? **c'est
  quoi en français, "friend"?**
school **le collège** m
  at school *au collège*

Scotland **l'Écosse** f
  in Scotland *en Écosse*
sea **la mer** f
seaside **au bord de la mer**
select **sélectionne**
second (2nd) **deuxième**
seventy **soixante-dix**
she **elle**
shop **le magasin** m
  to go round the shops **faire les magasins**
shy **timide** m or f
singer **chanteur** m, **chanteuse** f
sister **la sœur** f
sixty **soixante**
skateboarding **le skateboarding** m
  I go skateboarding **je fais du skateboarding**
skating rink **la patinoire** f
ski: I go skiing **je fais du ski**
small **petit** m, **petite** f
smell **l'odeur** f
snow **la neige** f
  it's snowing *il neige*
smoke: he smokes **il fume**
soap (TV): **la série** f
sofa **le canapé** m
some **des**
sometimes **parfois**
song **la chanson** f
soon **bientôt**
  see you soon *à bientôt!*
sorry **pardon**
Spain **l'Espagne** f
  to Spain *en Espagne*
speak: people speak French **on parle français**
spell: how do you spell it? **ça s'écrit comment?**
sport **le sport** m
sports centre **le centre sportif** m
sporty **sportif** m, **sportive** f
spring: in spring **au printemps**
stadium **le stade** m
stay: I stay (at home) **je reste (à la maison)**
stomach **l'estomac** m
  I have stomach ache **j'ai mal à l'estomac**
story **l'histoire** f
strawberry **la fraise** f
street **la rue** f
stupid **stupide, bête** m or f
subject: school subject **la matière** f
sugar **le sucre** m
  some sugar *du sucre*
summer: in summer **en été**
Sunday **dimanche**
supermarket **le supermarché** m
sweets **les bonbons** mpl
swimming: I go swimming **je fais de la natation**
swimming pool **la piscine** f

T

table tennis **le ping-pong** m
  I play table tennis *je joue au ping-pong*
take: I take **je prends**
tea **le thé** m
teacher **prof** m or f
ten **dix**
tennis **le tennis** m
  I play tennis *je joue au tennis*
text message **le texto** m
thank you (for) **merci** *(pour)*
that **ça**
the **le** m, **la** f, **les** pl
then **puis**
there is **il y a**
they **ils** m, **elles** f
third (3rd) **troisième**
thirsty: I'm thirsty **j'ai soif**
thousand **mille**
Thursday **jeudi**
time: at what time? **à quelle heure?**
to 1 *à* to the cinema *au cinéma* m, to the railway station **à la gare** f
  2 (with countries) *en* to France **en France**
  3 (to people, houses) *chez* I went to my uncle's *je suis allé(e)* **chez mon oncle**
toast: some toast (with) *du toast* m *(avec)*
together **ensemble**
tomorrow **demain**
too **also**
town **la ville** f
  big town *une grande ville*
Tuesday **mardi**
TV **la télé** f
  I watch TV *je regarde la télé*

U

uncle **l'oncle** m
understand: I don't understand **je ne comprends pas**
  I didn't understand **je n'ai pas compris**
usually **d'habitude, normalement**

V

very **très**
victim **la victime** f
video **la vidéo** f
video recorder **le magnétoscope** m
video shop **la vidéothèque** f
visited: I visited **j'ai visité**

W

Wales **le pays de Galles** m
  in Wales *au pays de Galles*
walk: I go walking **je fais des promenades**
want: I want **je veux**
water **l'eau** f

was: it was **c'était**
  it was boring *c'était barbant*
watch: I watch (TV) **je regarde (la télé)**
watched: I watched **j'ai regardé**
water **l'eau** f
we **nous**
weather **le temps** m
  what's the weather like? *quel temps fait-il?*
website **le site web** m
Wednesday **mercredi**
week **la semaine** f
well **bien**
went: **je suis allé** m, **je suis allée** f
  I went swimming *j'ai fait de la natation*
what **quoi**
  what did you do? *tu as fait quoi?*
  what's your address? *c'est quoi, ton adresse?*
  what is "know" in French? *c'est quoi en français, "know"?*
when **quand**
where **où**
which? **quel** m, **quelle** f
white **blanc** m, **blanche** f
who **qui**
why? **pourquoi?**
windy: it's windy **il fait du vent**
winter: in winter **en hiver**
with **avec**
  with me *avec moi*
won: I won **j'ai gagné**
  we won *on a gagné*
word **le mot** m
write: I write **j'écris**

Y

year **l'an** m
  I'm 14 years old *j'ai 14 ans*
  I'm in Year 9 *je suis en quatrième*
yellow **jaune** m or f
yes **oui**
yesterday **hier**
you 1 **tu** 2 **vous**
young **jeune** m or f
  young people *les jeunes* mpl
your **ton** m, **ta** f, **tes** pl
youth club **le club** m **des jeunes**

Z

zoo **le zoo** m

Common instructions in *Voilà! 3*

Phrases

ajoute des détails	add details
au passé	in the past tense
c'est quelle photo?	which photo is it?
c'est qui?	who is it?
c'est quoi en français?	what is it in French?
change le dialogue	change the dialogue
complète les phrases	complete the sentences
dans le bon ordre	in the right order
écoute et lis	listen and read
écoute et répète	listen and repeat
écris les mots	write the words
écris les phrases	write the sentences
écris tes réponses	write your own answers
en anglais	in English
en français	in French
expressions de temps	time phrases
fais deux listes	write two lists
joue le dialogue	act out the dialogue
joue et adapte le dialogue	act out and adapt the dialogue
lève la main	put your hand up
lis la lettre	read the letter
pose les questions à ton/ta partenaire	ask your partner the questions
recopie les mots	copy the words
regarde les images	look at the pictures
réécoute…	listen to… again
réponds aux questions	answer the questions
ton modèle, c'est…	the pattern for you to base your work on is…
trouve les paires	find the matching pairs
vérifie avec ton/ta partenaire	check with your partner
vrai ou faux?	true or false?

Single words

aussi	too, as well
autre(s)	other
avec	with
le bon	the right
la bonne	the right
change	change
chaque	each
choisis	choose
comment	how
complète	complete
corrige	correct
dans	in
décris	describe
devine	guess
le dialogue	the dialogue
discute	discuss
dit	says
écoute	listen
écris	write
une erreur	mistake
et	and
explique	explain
faux	false
l' image	the picture
un jeu	a game
joue	play, act out

la lettre	letter
lis	read
le mot	the word
un nom	a name
note	note down
l' option	option, alternative
ou	or
où	where
le passé	the past (tense)
la phrase	the sentence
pour	for
prononce	pronounce, say
puis	then
quel(s)	which / what
quelle(s)	which / what
qui	who
quoi	what
recopie	copy
réécoute	listen again
regarde	look at
relis	re-read
remplace	replace
répète	repeat
la réponse	the answer
trouve	find
vrai	true

Photo credits